MW00462198

FIRST LIGHT

FIRST LIGHT

A Magical Journey

CAROL O'BISO

Paragon House
New York

First American edition, 1989

Published in the United States by

Paragon House
90 Fifth Avenue
New York, NY 10011

This edition is published by arrangement with the
author and Heinemann Publishers (New Zealand).

Library of Congress Cataloging-in-Publication Data

O'Biso, Carol.
First light : a magical journey / Carol O'Biso. — 1st American ed.
p.   cm.
ISBN 1-55778-207-5
1. O'Biso, Carol—Journeys—New Zealand. 2. Museum registrars—
New York (N.Y.)—Biography. 3. New Zealand—Description and
travel—1981- 4. New York (N.Y.)—Biography. I. Title.
CT275.0216A3   1989
919.31'0437—dc19   89-3175
                                                                         CIP

Manufactured in the United States of America

The paper used in this publication meets the minimum requirements of
American National Standard for Information Sciences—Permanence of Paper
for Printed Library Materials, ANSIZ39.48-1984.

For Jamie, who continues to move my life; for Doris and Bernie, whose love and support have no human bounds; and for my parents, who taught me how to fly.

CONTENTS

	Acknowledgments	ix
	Author's Note	xi
1	The Beginning	1
2	The Ground	12
3	The Seed	70
4	The Plant	91
5	The Flower	125
6	The Fruit	181

ACKNOWLEDGMENTS

I'd like to thank Deborah Miller, who lovingly groomed this manuscript in its early stages; my running partners, Linda Stanley, Phyllis Haynes and Gene Martineau for listening to me mile after mile, and Sarah Jane Freymann for being wonderful as well as for being a good literary agent. Lesley and Kevin P. must also be thanked. They opened their home, their hearts and their lives and let me in. I'd especially like to thank the Maori people of New Zealand for giving me the privilege of taking care of their ancestors for four years of my life.

AUTHOR'S NOTE

I'm a New Yorker. I thought that meant I was prepared for anything but no one warned me about New Zealand. "Go," they said, "there's a job to be done." So I went. I haven't been the same since, but then New Zealand hasn't been the same either. We're both changed.

I live in New Zealand now. When this adventure started, I would have laughed if you'd suggested that. "Me? Live there? Don't be ridiculous!" I might even have sneered. I hated New Zealand that first time. You don't hear too many people say that, but I hated it.

An incredible series of events led up to my change of heart. Subtle and not so subtle, the events intrigued and amused, infuriated, and finally they got inside. Even during the first trip here, even while I was hating it, I began to change but couldn't really tell. I don't know how long I'll stay in New Zealand. After all, it's not New York (and I still miss New York), but some magical thing has pulled me back here.

I'll tell the story now and since New Zealand is a small country where word travels fast; since I thought my colleagues and friends might like to keep their privacy, I've changed their names. They'll know who they are and can say if they like. America is big. It swallows you whole and you can disappear if you want to. Those people can fend for themselves and so their real names have been used.

Welcome to my story.

ONE

The Beginning

I am young enough that some people still call me a girl. These are mostly men or my mother. Even I sometimes call myself a girl although I never do so out loud.

My hair is straight and dark brown. At one time, for a long time, I kept it shockingly long. Now it is equally short and resembles a long-needled pine.

Sometimes I am beautiful. This depends, it seems, on what I eat for breakfast or on the relative humidity in the air. The rest of the time I am ordinary.

When I came to New York I was afraid of the dark, the subways, of black people or of any people who were very different from me. I included nearly everyone in this category. I am still sometimes afraid of these things, only now I know that they are afraid of me too. Now I am also afraid of polyester clothes, of quiche and very often of croissants. I am terrified of Bloomingdale's.

I was raised a Catholic because my parents could not take a stand. Also they said that the schools were better.

I was raised in New Jersey for very fine reasons I have never questioned. New Jersey must simply be accepted.

I grew up Italian because my mother is from Milano; my father, Palermo. They met in America, in New Jersey.

My name is Carol. My life has been different from most. I try to explain this by sifting through the information. I look for clues but none emerge. There seems no reason. It is not because I am Italian. There are many of those. God knows it is not New Jersey. Many, in fact, are both Italian and from New Jersey with that combination still not producing the magic. There are, as well, countless lapsed Catholics. I am not lapsed. That is too passive a word to describe my relationship to the Church.

"Outside," said the nuns, "are Roman soldiers. They will poke sticks in your ears and cut out your tongues if you do not memorise your catechism." "In the playground," said the nuns to the creamy-faced, freckle-faced, pimple-faced little girls in solemn navy pleats, "is a yellow line. If you cross over that line to the little boys' side of the playground you will be pregnant. You will not be able to go home because your families will not have you, such bad little girls." We did not, most of us, know what pregnant meant. "If you sit on the church steps you will get kidney stones," said the nuns. We knew what stones were, used them to play hopscotch and skip-on-the-lake. We were unsure about kidneys.

Can history like this produce magic, then? Magic can easily be mistaken for coincidence and often it is wrongly called accident or luck. It is necessary to watch very carefully, to suspect absolutely everything of magic. Soon you can see that everything is.

I was to be a painter, but did not paint very well. This seemed to be a minor problem and mostly escaped notice entirely. I thought being a painter was a profession, like housepainter. I thought it was something one had a tendency towards, learned to do and became good at. I did not know that painter dancer cellist writer boiled in your blood looking for crevices from which to ooze into the world.

I was encouraged in the pursuit of becoming a painter because my parents were both artistic, but also counselled to be practical because my parents had lived through the war. Accordingly, I decided to become an art teacher. I would paint on the side.

It is possible that the decision was not actually mine. I do not specifically remember the conversations but it is possible that my parents, in the person of my mother, a schoolteacher who does all the conversing for both, engaged me in several conversations. It is likely that while I washed the dishes and she sponged the stove, my mother said how good it would be for me to be an artist since I had always shown considerable talent in that area. It is possible that as we folded sheets together she went on to say how important it was to consider ways of supporting myself and what a secure profession teaching was. Also that it would leave much free time. It is very possible that she said these things carefully and in such a way that I could choose, if I wanted, not to think I was being told what to do. I was at an age when more than anything I needed not to think I was being told what to do, especially by my parents.

It might be that we all then waited a sufficient amount of time for these conversations to be carefully forgotten. In that way, when I announced my decision I could be cool and offhand, only thinly camouflaging an immense pride in my independence. They could smile and be casual, looking briefly up from their eggs and only poorly hiding a fierce pride in the levelheadedness of their child. Everyone was pleased. Strangely, my sister also chose to become an art teacher. Marriage was never mentioned.

It might have been my dislike for children or that the magic had begun to work, I don't know; maybe both. There were the faces: disinterested faces, sullen faces, interested faces feigning disinterest for appearance's sake. Fourteen-year-old, seventeen-year-old, sometimes eighteen-year-old faces. Nearly all pimpled faces.

There were the legs; facing me, defiantly crossed or spread and slack. Corduroy crotches, denim crotches, panties showing, no panties showing; disinterested legs. Legs that wanted, always, to be elsewhere. There was Maggie, the teacher. "Call me Maggie," she said, and I was shocked because I had been taught never to call someone older Maggie. "This is Miss

O'Biso," she said to the class. "She will be our new practice teacher," and I was shocked because no one had ever called me Miss before.

Maggie sat at the back of the room and read novels for eight weeks. Occasionally she looked up with blank eyes. She smiled a lot at the end of each day, telling me what a good job I was doing and next morning came in and went back to her book. She had long since grown too weary although she was only forty-two. Maggie lived for weekends, summer vacation and as many practice teachers as she could legitimately get. She cried when I left. "I feel weepy," she said and hugged me at the car. I cried too, but only because I had seen this for the death that it was.

This is how you tell the difference between magic and death. Death is when you see death and you walk right into it because the other way is to look like a fool. Death is when you go on so long and try so hard not to look like a fool that it begins to resemble life. It is also where you take the time to carefully forget that once, for a moment, you could see clearly. This is death.

Magic is different. It is when you are a fool and know that you are probably not alone in this. Magic also has a lot to do with telling yourself the truth about the way things are. It doesn't matter who else you tell it to.

*   *   *   *   *

When I was twenty I found that I preferred the company of snakes to that of children. Now I have come to enjoy them almost equally, the snakes still holding a slight edge. This preference sent me, in panic-stricken flight, from the world of the classroom to that of museums where practice teaching requirements could be completed at a safe distance from a school. It was in museums that I was to discover who I was and what I was supposed to be doing.

This discovery began with the snakes, in particular Mora, the boa constrictor who was seven feet long and was heavy enough that when she was wrapped around my arm that hand had to be held against the wall for additional support; and the python, who was eight feet long and remained unnamed. He was aloof and had not succeeded in charming humans in quite the same way as Mora.

At first I was frightened when the woman from the museum handed me a snake. But the woman from the museum was, after all, not so very different from me. She was young and dark-haired, though mine was long and hers short and she, being just a few years older, made it possible to see that the only difference between us was that I was afraid and she was not. I was fascinated by my fear and by her lack of it. I was fascinated and for a moment was able to see that in this matter of fear, there were choices to be made.

So I stayed at the museum in New Jersey and after some weeks was able to forget that I had once been afraid. I counted Mora and the python, the other snakes, iguanas, racoons, ferrets, monkeys and the entire population of the live animal gallery as a group of extraordinary new friends. I forgot about my fear but never so much that I was unable to recognize it in the faces of the children, and more, in the faces of the teachers who brought the children to the museum. "Now I am going to show you a reptile," I would say, lifting out Mora or perhaps the small black king snake who had once bitten me over some silly thing, leaving both rows of his teeth embedded in my palm when he drew away. I would watch the small faces, tittering nervously on the bleacher seats. They would watch their teacher. They knew that from their teacher they would find out which response they were to choose. Their excited faces hovered between fear, wonderment and curiosity and from their teacher that day they learned that in this situation and all situations like it, the correct response is fear. Very soon after that they forgot that this had been a matter of choice at all and came to regard this one response as the natural order of things.

When I finished my talk they would go off to see the Indian gallery, the film on volcanoes, the modern paintings and the pottery. Then they would board their yellow bus, rowdy with excitement, and go back to their school, few of them knowing what it was they had really learned from the museum that day. They had learned a bit about art and a bit about geology. Many had learned something about animals. What they hadn't learned was that they were afraid and I was not and that I was not, after all, so very different from them.

By the time my practice teaching requirements were complete I had come to love the museum too much to leave. I remained as a volunteer and continued to divide my time between school and the snakes and the children. But soon money became important. It was not money itself that became important; my parents were generous enough. The need was for money that comes without all the real and imagined conditions that money has when given by parents who are generous. Consequently, I found myself a job. By some quirk of fate the job was not in New Jersey, which would have been the customary expectation, but in New York. So now I divided my time between school, the museum and the job in New York.

Ranking high among the things that frighten me is not knowing. That is not to say that I was not at first afraid of snakes, but that I was more afraid of how I might behave when handed a snake. Not of death, you see, but of what I might do on the way to it.

In view of this New York provided endless opportunity for fear. The Port Authority Bus Terminal alone was an extravaganza of not knowing. Two mornings a week I stepped off the bus and steeled myself for the shock of this grisly passage. Two mornings a week I left the building and found myself confronted as if for the first time by the assault of 42nd Street and 8th Avenue, a corner so horrible for its deviant humanity that it makes the bus terminal, with a large deviant population of its own, appear a haven.

The bus came to seem like a space shuttle in the days before those were invented. It carried me, in thirty minutes, from one world deep into another. I liked to think it was somewhere in the Lincoln Tunnel that the switch was made. When the bus crawled out on the other side of the river it was still possible to look back. The shoreline of New Jersey could still be clearly seen, large and close across the Hudson. What could not be seen was the wall; an invisible glass wall that allowed the passage of only the smallest thoughts.

So I travelled, two days a week, under the river to work in a linen and lingerie shop on Fifth Avenue, and if New Jersey was a world away from 42nd Street, 42nd Street was at least that remote from Fifth Avenue.

Mildred, the manager of the linen shop, was sixty or so and was coarse and fat. Mildred smoked and wore tight knitted dresses and must have been girdled from neck to knee. Her flesh never moved. Mildred's hair was carefully bleached and teased and carefully lacquered, and on all of this you could tell she had carefully spent a great deal of money. But nothing can be done to dress and adorn laughter and when Mildred laughed the money fell away. When Mildred laughed her mouth opened wide and her teeth showed, her tongue showed and whatever food she might have been chewing showed around her teeth. At those moments it was possible to see underneath the lacquering and the teasing. It was possible to see beneath the money and to know, when she laughed, who Mildred was.

We worked in a windowless basement where I filed papers and she talked a lot on the phone. "Good morning, honey," she'd say each day. "Good morning, Bessie, good morning, Loretta, Larry, Roy." Mildred was careful to call each of us honey or each of us by our name each and every time she spoke to show how friendly she was. Loretta and Bessie ironed the linens. Each day at noon they heated foil packets on their steam irons. Soon the smell of yesterday's pot roast blended with the basement smell of the milky fluid that was sprayed once a month for the roaches. These two smells blended with the smell of Mildred's cigarettes. Soon the smells blended so well that they became only one smell which represented all the horrible smells of the universe. Soon after that it was impossible any longer to tell whether it was a smell at all, or only a feeling.

Two flights above, at street level, the shop sold silk panties for $98 a pair. The saleswomen who worked there were called girls in spite of their advanced years and the women who shopped there were called Mrs. or Ma'am. Their names were names that everyone knew, even in New Jersey. All these people, both the ones above the ground and the ones below it, were more shocking and foreign to me than Mora and the black king snake with whom I spent another two days of my week.

Once I was settled and content I found that I would not have enough credits to graduate unless I left the museum in New Jersey and spent more time on course work. This distressed me greatly. I found that I lacked eight credits and one day soon after this discovery I found I could earn eight credits by working three days a week at a museum in New York. I called this coincidence.

So I left Mora and the black king snake and all my human friends at the museum in New Jersey and moved on to complete my study requirements at a museum in New York. I left them in sadness because at this museum there would be no snakes and no iguanas and in fact, no animals at all. I was certain that I had forsaken the magical for the practical and certain that life would never be that magical again.

I divided my time between the job in New York and the museum, and now I traveled five days a week under the river and through the invisible glass wall. I rode back and forth between two worlds and over time my shock at the one turned, and looking back, slowly became shock at the other.

I left home when I was twenty-three. "It's the commuting," I said to their ashen faces. "Port Authority is very dangerous." This they knew to be true because my father commuted too, and they digested it quickly because they saw what could not be changed. "It was the commuting," they were able to say later as if they agreed and might have thought of it themselves. "Port

Authority is very dangerous." With this, everyone was satisfied. The truth was never spoken.

On the night before the move I curled in the bed across the room from my sister and cried. Through the night I reviewed all the wonderful things that had happened over the years of lying curled in the bed across the room from my sister. I cried because I knew I was grown now and must leave and was certain that things would never be this wonderful again. When I awoke the next day my eyes were dry and I left.

Before long I fell deeply in love. I attributed this to the fact that I now had my own apartment. It was difficult to fall deeply in love while curled in the bed across the room from my sister. There were stuffed animals on the shelves that ringed the room I shared with my sister. We had long since ceased to be aware of the animals that ringed the room, but still, it is difficult to fall deeply in love when each night you sleep under the gaze of stuffed animals in a room that you share with your sister.

I fell in love with a beautiful, gentle, older man. He was really much older and had beautiful hands and a kind and wonderful face. In addition to a kind and wonderful face he had a gentle voice. In addition to a gentle voice he had a wife and three children. At first the older man and I pretended that we were in love and soon it was true that we were in love. Then we pretended that we weren't in love and when we could no longer pretend, we parted. This process took two years.

The museum had, by now, become my life. It was a source of wild and extraordinary adventures and it was adventures that had become my life. But at last I graduated and it came time to find a job. I prepared to leave this museum that was now my life, and I was stricken and sorrowful. On the day before I was to leave, the museum offered me a job. I called this incredible luck. Still I did not suspect magic.

Ranking high among the things that excite me is knowing. So I stayed at the museum in New York. I stayed four years at this museum because, though it was small, there was much to learn. I came to know that there was joy in pushing to the limits of what could be done, and freedom in finding no limits to what could be done. At this museum I found out how much I could lift, how late into the night I could work, how many things it was possible to do at once and how little money I could manage to live on. Soon I also came to know something about people. I learned about people who were black or brown or Jewish and about people who were old. I found out about people who had grown up very rich, about people who had grown up very poor and about all those people I included in the category of being very different from me. Soon I was able to see that in spite of grave differences in the way we looked, where we came from and in the way we lived, we were not so very different at all.

The most important thing I learned while at this museum was about limits and what they had to do with people. Sometimes one of the people smiled or one of them laughed. Often one of them said something very funny and very rude about the lateness of the hour or the weight of the load. Sometimes one of them said, "I will go for the pizza tonight because you went last night," and often we all just looked at each other in the middle of something tedious and smiled.

It was at those times that there were no limits. At those times it was possible to lift also the four-by-eight sheets of plywood, possible to carry them up three flights of stairs instead of two. It was possible to work, not late into the night, but through the night and it was possible to do this several nights in a row. Soon it was easy to do even greater numbers of things all at the same time and to laugh in delight while doing them. On days when I worked alone I tired very early.

Here is how you know when it is time to leave. It is time to leave when a voice says, "It is time to leave," and you go through the motions as if this were true. When you do this and nothing gets in your way and over the proper course of time you do leave, then it is time. It is not time to leave when you say, "I am going to leave," and you go through the motions as if this were true, finding nothing but walls and in the walls nothing but doors and all of them locked. Then it is not time to leave yet.

For a year I thought it was time to leave because it seemed there was little left to learn. For a year I found nothing but walls. I struggled against them from time to time because it is important to test these walls to see that they are not just your own fears disguised as walls. After a year I no longer had to struggle to leave. I was fired instead. "You have been terminated," the director said to nineteen of us one day. "There is no money to meet the August payroll." In two days we were gone, our desk drawers empty and the surfaces clean. Three days after that I had a new job. I called this luck too.

The job I moved to took me, not under the river, but around the world. In this job I was called a registrar and after two years, chief registrar. In this job, works of art of staggering value and jarring beauty were placed in my care. These works of art travelled from museum to museum around the world and as they travelled I travelled too. I travelled to San Francisco and Detroit, to New Orleans, Denver and Des Moines. I travelled to Tokyo, to London and in all of these places, it took greater and greater twists of the mind to see that the people were not so very different from me.

The job asked a great deal, but I was willing, and in return it took me on all manner of wild and exciting adventures in all sorts of wild and exotic ways. After five years it took me to New Zealand. In New Zealand, all that I'd learned about fear and about limits and all that I'd learned about people was tested and stretched and tested again until it exploded. In New Zealand I finally began to suspect magic.

Here is what I know about magic. Magic is when all the hard things and all the easy things and all the things that happen to you at all begin to look as if they were planned. Magic is when you behave as if all the things that happen to you were planned even when it doesn't look that way. This is magic.

TWO

The Ground

George:

"New Zealand? No kidding? We heard on the radio last week
. . . did you hear about this? . . . that they just discovered a
primitive tribe in the jungle there who have never seen a white
man. They don't even know it's the twentieth century. God, New
Zealand! That's really great, kid."

"No, I didn't hear about it, George, but I think maybe you
mean New Guinea."

"No, I'm sure it was New Zealand. They said this tribe still
practices cannibalism and . . ."

"George, there are no primitive tribes in New Zealand. The
country isn't big enough. There are no unexplored territories.
George, they wear suits in New Zealand."

"Oh, well, I guess maybe you're right. But I was sure . . .
Oh, well, now that I think about it, no, oh, I guess maybe they
did say New Guinea. Anyway, when are you going?"

A Trustee at an office cocktail party:

"I understand the May-or-ee are very friendly people. I've
always loved their art. John and I bought a carving for our
collection when we were there in '74."

"Really? How long were you there, and by the way, I believe they call themselves Maoris. That's *Mow-ree.*"

"Oh yes, of course. We were there for two weeks and we've loved May-or-ee art ever since."

My Aunt Mary:

"New Zealand! How wonderful, dear. You remember Uncle Herb and Aunt Ann went to Australia last year and they loved it."

"Yes, I remember, Aunt Mary. But they're two different places, you know."

"What, dear? Oh, yes. Well, I'm sure you'll have fun. Aunt Ann said the kangaroos were adorable. They went to a place where the animals came right up and ate out of your hand."

A friend:

"You remember Joanne? She and her husband saved and dreamed all of their lives to retire to New Zealand. When they both retired and applied to emigrate they found out you can't move there if you're over 40. They were devastated."

"Jesus! Is that true? I've never heard that before. I wonder why? Maybe they don't want it to become the Miami of the South Pacific."

Nearly everyone:

"Do they speak English there?"

"Most of them don't speak anything but."

Nearly everyone else:

"Mallory??"

"No, that's Maori-*Mow-ree.* You know, the indigenous people of New Zealand. Like the American Indian here. I'm going down to work on an exhibition of Maori art that will tour the United States."

"Oh, right. What do Mow-oo-ree Indians look like?"

"Oh, well, sort of Polynesian, never mind."

The cab driver on the way to JFK Airport:

"New Zealand! Did you hear a few months back they found a primitive tribe there that eat people? Cannibals, they call 'em."

"Yes, someone told me about that. But you know, I think you mean New Guinea."

"You think so? I thought the guy said New Zealand."

"That's okay. So did my brother-in-law, George."

       *   *   *   *   *

Here is what I know. If there were any other fast way to get there, anywhere, I would never get on an airplane again. "New Zealand," the ad says. "Beautiful New Zealand, only sixteen hours away." Maybe eighteen, something like that. What they don't tell you is that this is true only if the plane you take from New York flies right up and inserts itself into the one you switch to in Los Angeles, which already has a rolling start down the runway; that one lands in Honolulu where a ground crew chases it down with fuel hoses while it coasts from a landing into the take-off, the wheels never stopping. Because otherwise it takes 32 hours. Door to door. My behind, when I leave L.A., is conical, has taken on the shape of the moulded plastic seats. The only economical connection is the one that has me pinned in L.A. for six hours. There are better airports for this. When I leave Honolulu my eyelids are fluttering from fluorescent lights and exhaustion.

It is dark outside but they serve breakfast. There have also been a lunch, two dinners and a snack. I pass some time trying to detect a pattern. I give up. For one of the dinners they serve duck. This is very unusual, and so is the duck. Must have been a mallard, anyway something wild or something that has flown nonstop from New Zealand. Most muscular duck I've eaten.

The plane is packed. The man next to me talks for two hours while I nod and smile. I think my face will break. Finally he falls asleep and his neck goes to rubber, his head dipping, occasionally onto my shoulder. I massage my face to get the smile off. My own companion, a woman colleague of about 35, has hardly spoken since New York.

When we get to Auckland it is 6:40 A.M. their time. On a Friday. I think I remember leaving New York on a Monday, but I don't question this. They said it would be a little screwy and besides, considering the way I look and feel, it is not hard to believe that I might have been flying for four days. I might be wrong. I am very tired.

We are met by a man I have met, thank God, once before in New York at a meeting when things were just getting organized. No one has to wear a carnation or hold up a sign saying Queen Elizabeth II Arts Council. I recognize him immediately even though I was afraid I wouldn't. He is very white and soft and looks British. I introduce him to my colleague and we all begin to move through the hugging, laughing crowd toward the glass doors outside which the man says he has left his car. No matter what I do I can't keep my bags from getting between my legs, tripping me. My pants are being dragged down around my knees. The man sees this and takes another of my bags. "I am a professional," I say to myself. "I am the registrar of a major United States arts organization. I am here on important business." I say this again, trying to see if there is any chance I can make myself believe it. I pray there are no mirrors between here and the car.

My colleague strolls proudly with her green Samsonite suitcase. It is no bigger than my document case and weighs half. "I never take more than I can carry easily," she has said. I can tell that this is something of a religion for her so I back off. Never mess with somebody's religion. "We will be here six weeks," I think, wondering if what she has in the suitcase is like a futuristic pill that supplies all your nutritional needs. Sprinkle water on it and it turns into an entire wardrobe. At the same time

I know that, once again, I have overpacked. The dynamic that is set up between us at that moment is somehow one of competition. I take note of this and am concerned. It is no way to start.

When we get to the car I stand by the passenger door waiting for the man to get in the other side and unlock the doors. I do this until I notice that he is smiling and that there is a steering wheel on my side. "I remember this," I think. "I've driven in London."

I walk around the car and a car almost hits me because I am looking the other way. I insist that my colleague take the front seat. This looks like gallantry, but is really selfishness. "I'll take you to your hotel now so you can freshen up," the man says. "Freshen up?" I think. I want to die. "Oh, thank you," I say and laugh. "We are a bit tired." "Yes," he says, "quite." It sounds to me as if he has something in his nose. "We've scheduled a meeting for noon," he says. The man doesn't speak very loudly and tends to mumble a bit but I think I've heard correctly. "A meeting at noon?" I say perkily. "Yes, just a brief one. There are a few issues we need to discuss." "Of course," I say. "That's fine."

I fall back now and let my colleague in the front seat make small talk about the countryside. I spend the rest of the ride thinking how not-fine that is. This is how my trip begins.

*   *   *   *   *

October 29, 1982, Auckland, N.Z.

Everyone
The American Federation of Arts
New York, U.S.A.

Dear everyone,

I've decided it's healthier to be amused by our hotel rather than disappointed. "Do you see," I said to Cap, "that we have flown 12,000 miles to a Best Western Motor Lodge?"

They've booked us together in a double room. This is a bit

odd by American business standards but I don't mind and assume Cap doesn't either.

I won't say our first meeting went well. Cap and I had just arrived and had been up for two days. It was me, Cap, Matthew Sutterman and Peta Andrei (pronounced *Pay-ta,* by the way). Peta is young and looks more Italian than I do. Not at all what I expected a Maori to look like. Apparently there really is an Italian lurking way back in his ancestry. Anyway, it's clear they don't know what a registrar is.

I made my usual speech, the one that goes, "My responsibilities are the care and handling of the works of art. If you have any questions about the packing, transportation, insurance, climatic requirements, conservation or fumigation of the objects I would be the best one to talk to." They did have questions about those things. They had enough questions to keep this "brief" meeting going for an hour and a half over lunch and another half hour back in our hotel room. The problem was all the questions they had about other stuff. I said I was not prepared to discuss loan dates, the publication or the status of our funding, since I have only a general knowledge of those things. They nodded their heads but it seemed to me they just kept asking the same questions in different words.

I tried to divert some of their questions to Cap, saying that she had been hired by us to act as the U.S. Conservator, that her role would specifically be to inspect all of the objects and determine whether they are fit to travel or would need treatment. There were no questions about that, of course, because Matthew and Peta don't know much, if anything, about conservation and Cap hasn't seen any of the objects yet. Nice try, anyway.

Worst of all was the food. Peta said Bluff oysters are the best in the world. Only problem was, these had been frozen. They were brown and smelled like ammonia. It is a lot to expect anyone to eat rotten oysters, but it is especially a lot to expect of someone who has not slept in a bed in 42 hours. I ate one and had to carefully search my brain to see if there was any way I could get the rest down in the interest of international diplomacy. There was not. Matthew was looking at me kind of funny because I had said I was starving, but now was not eating. "I'm sorry," I said, "but I don't think I can eat these."

I expected the entire exhibition to go up in smoke over a goddamned oyster. He was, however, more than sympathetic and had the waiter take them away. I was so relieved I thought I was going to cry or that my head was going to explode.

At one point, as we were discussing our itinerary, I said, "By the way, Peta, where can we get a detailed road map? All I have is this very simplified tourist one from the consulate." He looked at the map in front of me on the table. "That *is* a detailed map," he said. "There are no other roads." His expression never changed.

When the meeting was over (finally), Matthew said they were taking us on a tour of Auckland. "Really!" I said. I said this perkily but it was unclear whether I meant "Lovely!" or "Are you kidding!?" This was deliberate. I was feeling him out. I caught Cap's eye and she just shrugged in surrender. He drove us around pointing out God knows what and we made all the right appreciative noises. Just as we were finally climbing out of the car back at the Barrycourt Motor Lodge, Peta said a man from Maori Affairs would be by to take us sightseeing in the morning. "Oh," I said. It was all I could manage.

Cap and I fell in the door of our room, almost frantic to get to bed. That's when the phone rang. "This is Bill Something-or-other," a man's voice said. I didn't get the last name. It was a strange voice, raspy and a bit silly. He giggled. I thought maybe it was a practical joke, but I was thinking the whole thing was a practical joke by then. "From Maori Affairs," he said. Oh yes, of course, our weekend guide. "I'll be by to get you girls at 7:00 tomorrow," he says. "You're at the Barrycourt, eh?" I was stunned. "Seven o'clock! In the morning!?"

He giggled again but somehow I knew it wasn't because he was kidding. Cap had gotten the gist of the conversation and was looking a little glazed. I bargained him down to 9:00 and asked where we were going. I tried to sound interested and eager, which was becoming increasingly difficult. "Oh, up north," he says. "Plenty to see up north." And just as he's about to hang up he says, "We'll get you girls back in plenty of time on Sunday." "Sunday! Are we staying up north overnight?" "Plenty of relations up north," Bill giggles. "We'll find someone to stop with." When I got off the phone I looked at Cap and said, "I think they're trying to kill us." "Gee," she said. "Gee." We fell into the beds.

Bill is on his way here now. I'll write again when we return from this adventure.

Love to all,
Carol

October 31, 1982, Auckland, N.Z.
The American Federation of Arts
New York, U.S.A.

Dear folks,

When last heard from we were about to head north for the weekend. Bill was late which was okay because so was the woman from Avis delivering our rental car. Bill arrived with Cheryl. "This is Cheryl," he said and giggled. He bent down and gave us each a big kiss. I have stopped listing the things that are a bit odd by American business standards. Cheryl is maybe 30, extremely beautiful and cocoa-skinned. Tall and slim. She smiled and said hello so softly it was hard to know she had spoken.

Bill looks about 45 and is very large. Everything about him was very large except his shirt, which was too small; a wild Hawaiian print with a great deal of his belly poking out from under. He is darker skinned than Cheryl but with the same jet-black hair. His had been greased, or possibly just not washed, and rippled back glassily along the sides of his head. "You're Cap and you're Carol," he said, jabbing a huge finger in confirmation of the introductions. When he said it it sounded like *Kep* and *Kerol*. "That's right," we smiled. He giggled. Cheryl just looked. "Let's take your car," Bill said. "It's bigger." He and Cheryl walked towards the station wagon from Avis. We watched their backs and looked at each other, fascinated by the possibilities.

Nothing really bad happened when Bill fell asleep at the wheel. We got a little scared. The side of the car got a little scraped on the rock wall when we bounced off it a few times. Cap did well. She was on that side of the car and didn't scream or anything. Bill jerked the wheel back and forth. "She got away from me," he said and mumbled something about the steering column.

He jerked the wheel from time to time during the next twenty minutes to prove that there was something wrong with the car. No one said anything like, "You don't think you could have fallen asleep for a minute there, do you Bill?" Nothing like that. Soon the steering column got better by itself.

Our nerves were a little jangled and the silence in the car was sort of thick. I was desperate to get out, if only briefly, and get my wits back around me. It was funny to now be thinking of ways to get him to make a stop. The morning had been spent doing the reverse. The first time Bill stopped that morning it was the steak pies. He never asked us if we wanted them, just pulled up to a small storefront and disappeared inside. He came back with a grease-stained paper bag and handed out these fat, flaky pies. They were still hot and were quite good if you like meat and in particular if you like your meat at 10:00 A.M. I just wished I had skipped breakfast.

The second stop was juice. As before, he just went inside without saying anything and handed out waxed cartons of bizarre colored juices when he came back. Half an hour later he pulled up to a whitewashed, concrete building that said "Dairy" over the door. I got a little nervous. He came back clutching three vanilla cones in one hand, and already licking a fourth. One was running down his hand and the other two down each other. He put an enormous hand in the back window for me to extract one. "Gee, Bill, this is awfully nice of you," I said, "but I don't think I can eat much more." I laughed a little, you know, to show that I wasn't being unappreciative. He just giggled, a rasping wheezing giggle. What are you supposed to do with an ice cream cone you don't want? Save it for later?

Now, I stood the tension as long as I could, watching him jerk the wheel around. "I have to go to the bathroom," I finally said. Bill giggled. I didn't take it personally. "We'll be stopping soon," he said. "Some relations up here a little way. They'll get us some lunch." Oh God.

His relations, cousins I think he said, lived in an extremely dirty farmhouse at the end of a long gravel road. They weren't there, in fact it looked as if no one had been there in years, but the door was open and we went in anyway. Bill went right to the refrigerator, not an entirely surprising move on his part. He found only a head of lettuce which he ate, leaf by leaf, including the considerable amount of garden soil still clinging to the leaves.

Well, this could get boring, this tale of torture, because it goes on a good bit longer. Here are some of the highlights. The relations we "stopped" with were Dan and Amy, who operate a dairy farm. Later I found out that Dan is a very big deal politically although I never did get the particulars straight. He took us on a tour of the farm, which was quite interesting. They crop the cows' tails here! They look awful, like amputees, wagging their little stumps, helpless against the flies. Dan said it was for sanitary reasons, but I can't figure it. Mostly we all just sat in front of the TV. There was a very brief dinner of micro-waved snapper, boiled beef and greens followed by more TV. Cap and I got the "girl's" rooms, where we were comfortable but lay awake because below us someone was playing the Grateful Dead all night. Bill walked into our room at ten to seven on Sunday morning to see if we wanted to go to Ninety Mile Beach! We declined. Too far. "Gee," Cap said when he left, "doesn't anyone ever sleep around here?" I suspect not.

Being awake all night at least gave me time to cook up a plot
to get Bill out from behind the wheel. "Listen, Bill," I said over
a cup of tea. "I've been thinking it would be good if Cap and I
had a chance to get used to the right-hand-drive car while you're
still around to coach us. How about we drive home?" We shared
six hours of driving back to Auckland. Bill snored in the back
seat the whole way.

You might say it was a stressful weekend. I'll write again
soon.

Love,
Carol

       *   *   *   *   *

Several times during the first night they let me sleep, this
thought comes to mind: "Things are going badly." I reject it.
"Things are not going badly," I say and fall back, thickly, into
sleep. "It will be fine. I will do well." I slide in and out of sleep,
in and out of dreams.

In the morning I have forgotten. There is sunshine and the air
is cool. I stare in wonder out the window because I know it is
spring and because I know also that it is October. There is no
way of telling which to believe. Just to be sure I fill the sink and
let the water out quickly, watching to see which way it spirals.
They say it goes down the other way here. I realize that I have
never noticed any consistency in the way it drains at home and
wonder why I tried this.

For breakfast there is tea, thick as stew, black as ink. "Bring
hot water," I say, "I cannot drink this," and pour one quarter tea
to three quarters water and drink this, with toast and jam. For
breakfast there is also canned spaghetti in tomato sauce. I watch
people ladle it from chafing dishes onto their toast; baked beans
onto their toast; fried eggs with curled edges, the yolks gone
opaque; sausages, orange juice of too bright a color and slippery a texture. I eat my white toast and drink the black tea,

watching in horror and delight. I decide to save these strange adventures for another day.

I drive to work with my colleague and when we get there I am embarrassed because the museum is huge. It is built of massive grey stones and sits alone atop a hill in the park. It overlooks the sea. I realize that my subconscious was expecting a hut.

We are met by a man who has longish grey hair and wears socks with his sandals. He is a curator and has written scholarly books on subjects that interest minute fragments of the world's population. I have not read these books. He leads us down a corridor that rings the museum. The corridor is dark and the smells are smells that say nothing has changed here in a century. When we come to a window, what is pretty about Auckland flashes before us.

I stare in wonder as the sea explodes with light and white sails. Then it is gone. We pass green metal cabinets and battered boxes covered with dust. The linoleum floor is brown. There is another explosion of sea and sails and then the man turns a corner and follows the hallway down a different face of the building. I anticipate the next window but still I am dazzled. On this side Rangitoto Island floats, stark and elegant on a flashing sea. Interrupted visions. Beauty and the Beast. We follow the man through claustrophobic tunnels until he turns again, this time away from the outer corridor to one that cuts deep into the center of the building. We follow, leaving what is pretty about Auckland behind.

He uses his key to open a small door cut into a bigger one and steps through. I am excited now because I am about to see what it is I have come all this way to see. We step through the door behind him. The room is dimly lit and is so small and the ceiling so high that it appears somehow to be a room stood on end. I wait for my eyes to adjust to the dimness of one flickering fluorescent tube twenty-five feet above.

The room appears to be filled with lumber. Odd-shaped planks lie on the floor and lean against the walls. I am stricken with discouragement, wondering how we are going to work in this place. "I guess you'll need another light," the man says.

I think how we will need a lot more than that. I don't say this. The man goes and when he returns he has a bare bulb on an eight-foot cord. He climbs over some of the lumber to get to a plug. When the glaring light goes on, I see that it is not lumber at all, but some of the artifacts from the exhibition. I am careful not to let my expression change.

I look around now and realize that the things leaning on the wall are also objects for the exhibition. I try to look up, to see the top of them, but the bare bulb has made too much contrast between dark and light. The carvings vanish at about twelve feet into the shadows. I feel wild, hysterical laughter building up in my throat but I turn calmly to the man and say, "A ladder would be nice." This is a small, silly thing to say but I can think of nothing else. He goes again and when he returns he is carrying a six-foot ladder. I almost look down at the ladder and then up at the carvings, but don't because I feel this would be rude. Instead I smile ambiguously and say thank you. I know that my first day at work has begun.

*   *   *   *   *

November 1, 1982, Auckland, N.Z.
The American Federation of Arts
New York, U.S.A.

First day at work:

Dear all,

Our work space at the Auckland Institute is grim, grim, grim.

It took us until about noon to round up some extra lights and some of the smaller objects. I guess we can get started on those until I figure out how in hell we're going to deal with the big ones. What with morning tea at 10:00 and lunch at noon and afternoon tea at 3:00, it's a wonder anything at all happened today. Surprisingly, we managed to get a fairly good system going. I still don't know quite what to do about John Greet. "The New Zealand Conservator," Peta said. *What* New Zealand Conservator!? Did any of you know about a New Zealand Conservator? "He's just been appointed," Peta said. "He'll be working with you." Doing what, I wonder? Anyway, he isn't here yet. He called while we were at breakfast to say that he's still in Wellington because his flight is fogged in. I have at least until tomorrow to figure out something for him to do.

All we really did today was devise a system for how to locate, identify, inspect and photograph the objects. That was all we got to do because somewhere in between all the breaks and lunching and hunting for gear a Maori Anglican Minister came by to officially welcome us. He is small and round and brown, about 50 I'd guess, and very nice. He has invited us to a rehearsal of what he calls his "Cultural Group." I didn't quite get what that's all about, but we're going anyway.

To be continued . . .

'Bye for now,

Carol

Cap:

"Yes, I've read the paper this morning."

"Did you see this headline? 'Maori Artifacts Valued at $U.S. 27,000,000 to Tour America!' Where could they have gotten that!? That reporter badgered me for half an hour yesterday and I wouldn't tell him the value of the show."

"I bet somebody at the Auckland Institute told him."

"You're right. They're the only ones that could have had . . ."

"Why do you care anyway?"

"Oh, it's just bad for security, that's all. I don't want the whole country to know $U.S. 24,000,000—he was $3 million off—worth of stuff is going to be out there moving around in trucks. Damn reporters!"

The hotel clerk:

"You're celebrities! We saw you on the front page this morning."

"Yes, I was a little surprised myself. I didn't realize this was going to be such a big deal."

The waiter at the hotel restaurant:

"Are they really worth $27 million American dollars?"

"No, that's not true at all. I don't know where they got that figure."

"How much are they worth, then."

"I'm sorry, I can't say."

                                            November 2, 1982, Auckland, N.Z.

The American Federation of Arts
New York, U.S.A.

Dear all,

John Greet showed up today. There was a good bit of awkwardness about his role in this whole thing. I was kind of hedging around trying to get him to say what it is he needs to accomplish while he was hedging around waiting for me to tell him how he fits into our plans. This, of course, is the result of there never having been a plan to have a New Zealand Conservator.

In any case, after the initial awkwardness it turned out to be a good thing he was there today. I had planned to do all the condition photography myself, but things are incredibly disorganized. My time is completely occupied with tracking down the objects, which are either in our workroom, the adjacent schoolroom, or buried in prehistoric storage chambers. Once I find it, identify it, measure it and make notes on anything I'll need to know later to plan the packing, I hand it over to Cap, who inspects it and prepares the condition report. She points out to me and John anything that is especially dangerous or otherwise noteworthy and John takes the condition photos, paying particular attention to those areas. It works. Everyone is happy.

Love,
Carol

P.S. Can somebody do something about maybe getting Douglas's title changed? "The objects for the exhibition were selected by Douglas Newton, Chairman of the Department of Primitive Art at the. . . . ."

"Why are you people still using that word?" somebody always interrupts. I must admit, I've taken to mumbling a lot. It's hard to say "primitive art" to the primitive himself— especially when the primitive in question is wearing a three-piece suit!

P.P.S. Will you do me a favor and collect all my letters after they've made the rounds through the office? I have a feeling I'll enjoy reading them one of these days. I've written a few cards and letters to family and friends but it's too hard. They don't know the cast of characters. I'd rather just write to all of you at the office.

November 5, 1982, Auckland, N.Z.

Jamie Summers
New York, U.S.A.

Dear Jamie,

Things are sort of crazy here. I've been "looking" hard for some evidence to support your theories about the Maori people. None so far. They seem to be a fairly normal range of people, and not particularly spiritual or intuitive or anything. Things are very much dominated by the practical aspects of this journey right now, though. You might say I'm not exactly receptive to subtleties. I'll send you another card or a letter soon.

Love,
Carol

November 5, 1982, Gisborne, N.Z.

The American Federation of Arts
New York, U.S.A.

Hi everyone,

I now realize that there is a very important role for John in this exhibition. We've had two and a half work days in Auckland, one in Whakatane and now one in Gisborne and I don't know how Cap and I would have managed with only the two of us.

On the other hand, it is a bit stressful spending every waking moment with two people you hardly know and I'm sure it's no easier for Cap and John than it is for me. We are together for breakfast, lunch and dinner, all day at work and all day in the car while we're getting from place to place. I've started running again in spite of my sore throat. (I've tried to ignore it but the damn thing has persisted through ten days of antibiotics! Take these and get plenty of rest, my doctor said two days before I left home. Fat chance.) Anyway, the running gives me a whole hour out of twenty-four to myself and sometimes on a beautiful beach at that.

We're leaving for Wellington now so I must sign off.

Love,
Carol

P.S. The Whakatane Museum is about the size of the bathroom at the Auckland Institute. It looks a bit like a one-room schoolhouse with a staff of one: the director.

A Maori elder:

"These are the girls from the Metropolitan Museum."

"Good morning. Pleased to meet you, but actually we're not from the Metropolitan Museum."

"Oh? Where are you from, then? I understood that the exhibition was going to the Metropolitan Museum."

"Yes, that is so, but the Met is only the first exhibitor on the tour. The exhibition is being organized by the American Federation of Arts in New York and I am their Chief Registrar. Cap Sease has been hired by us to act as the U.S. Conservator."

"Oh, I see."

A museum curator:

"Would you be the girls from the Metropolitan Museum, then?"

"No, everyone seems to be quite confused about that. We're really from the American Federation of Arts in New York."

"Really? That is confusing."

"Yes, I know. I'm sure the fact that the exhibition's guest curator, Douglas Newton, is the Chairman of the Department of Primitive Art at the Met and the fact that Cap Sease worked at the Met for a number of years only confuses the issue further."

Another Maori elder:

"So how long have you girls been with the Metropolitan Museum?"

"We haven't or rather, Cap used to be but isn't any longer. I never worked for the Met. I am the Registrar at the AFA. We are the ones organizing the exhibition."

"Oh, what a pity that it won't be going to the Met, then."

A museum director:

"So you girls have come all the way from the Metropolitan Museum to look at our artifacts?"

"Uh, yes, that's right . . . Where are the restrooms, please?"

Cap:

"Do you think there's any way we can get them to stop calling us girls? It's making me crazy!"

"I wouldn't count on it."

*   *   *   *   *

November 9, 1982, Wellington, N.Z.
The American Federation of Arts
New York, U.S.A.

Hello all!

Time for another report. We are now in Wellington, called the Windy City, and they are not kidding around. No one warned me that it is a very bad idea to wear a full skirt here. I spent most of the first day keeping mine from flapping up around my ears. It is hard to look dignified when you are doing this, but it's also dangerous for other reasons. You need to keep your wits about you at all times to keep from being blown against a wall by the sudden gusts in the middle of an already fierce wind.

The other day I had to stop quite suddenly on the street and yank my earrings off! The wind was causing the copper danglers to flap around, madly hacking at the sides of my head. Our hotel room is on the fifth floor—a mistake. The wind has not stopped shrieking, howling and rattling the windows for days, and soon I will jump off the roof. If you can imagine such a thing, we have to fly out of there next week and I'm already working myself into a state of hysteria about it. Charming little town, really.

It's hard to believe it's November and Christmas is about the farthest thing from my mind in spite of traces of it in the shops. The real push here is for summer instead. Stores are displaying bathing suits and barbecue equipment, sailboats and patio furniture. There is an occasional Santa Claus thrown in as an after-thought, and they're sweating in the sun in those costumes. It's all very bizarre.

Yesterday morning, our first day at work here, there was a "transfer" ceremony in the great Maori hall at the National Museum. There have been ceremonies at each of the museums so far, with the exception of Auckland, but they were all rather vague and confused. In each case the local elders were on hand for our arrival. We'd gather, along with the museum staff which was usually one or two people, in some tiny storage room or office space. The elders would shuffle around and someone would make a welcome speech and then they'd all talk in Maori, trying to figure out what should happen next. Finally there'd be some prayers (real Christian stuff—Our Fathers and the like, which surprised me in the middle of a Maori ceremony) and then we'd all have tea together.

The ceremony here in Wellington, however, was very formal and also very moving. There is a large Maori meeting house in the great hall of the museum. On Monday morning there was a row of chairs in front of it (an area called the marae) for the museum director and about five Maori men. Across the hall, which is very large, were four chairs facing the meeting house. These were for me, Cap, John and Peta, who was to be our Maori representative. As we were led into the hall one of the older Maori women began a wail. "Haere mai!" (welcome) she called, in a high-pitched, slightly off-key wail that dragged the phrase on and on so that by the time she was done the word was echoing and careening around the room and up into what looked like thirty-foot ceilings. It gave me goose bumps.

When she finished all the men together shouted "Haere mai!" as well, and theirs was short, quick and powerful. Then there were formal speeches in Maori and English with both Peta and John speaking for our side. (This is the one point that really gets me. According to Maori custom women are not allowed to speak during these ceremonies. Cap and I must remain silent.)

At that point, something extraordinary began to happen. Throughout the ceremony thus far there had been a small carving, one of the ancestral figures for the exhibition, standing on the floor in front of the Maori side. Now, one at a time the men began to chant in Maori. One would come forward and move the figure, which is about fourteen inches high, a few feet across the great hall. Without pause, the next would pick up the

chant and come forward, moving the ancestor a few feet farther
out. This went on until it had reached the middle of the great
hall, at which point they nodded to Peta. He picked up the chant
and went out to meet the ancestor in the middle of the hall. He
picked it up and with it cradled in his arms began to walk slowly
back towards us, never losing the chant. He placed it gently in
Cap's arms like a baby, signifying the transfer to our care.

This was essentially the end of the ceremony. The room was
as still as the middle of the night. You could almost hear the
electricity crackle across the space. As we filed out of the great
hall on our way to tea there was a "receiving line" of sorts and
we were expected to bump noses twice, Maori style, with each
of the people on the line. We all went into the boardroom then
for tea and sandwiches and gradually everyone loosened up and
began to talk and laugh.

It has been an amazing experience to be in a country where
the spiritual well-being of the objects is a standard part of the
museum day. These are all modern, western people wearing
suits. It's hard to believe.

We leave here on Saturday morning and I'm really looking
forward to it. It will be the first time since our arrival that we get
a weekend to ourselves. Cap and I will take the ferry to the
South Island and spend Saturday and Sunday exploring the
Tasman Mountains. John will meet us there at the museum in
Nelson on Monday morning.

More news soon,
Carol

November 9, 1982, Wellington, N.Z.

Jamie Summers
New York, U.S.A.

Jamie!
We went through our first really formal ceremony today and it
was extraordinary. It isn't so much what was said or done, but

the amazingly powerful *energy* that filled the room. I had goose bumps through the whole thing.

Sorry, no time to write more now, but I'll have lots to tell when I get home.

Love,
Carol

November 10, 1982, Wellington, N.Z.
The American Federation of Arts
New York, U.S.A.

Hi there,

Things have been difficult.

I am exhausted from being a diplomat—never my forté to begin with. Occasionally I relax a bit and think things are going fine, start just enjoying the people. Invariably someone with flaring nostrils and hands on their hips says something like, "Why aren't the couriers going to be from our museums?" Then I have to pull my diplomat disguise back on and say, "That hasn't been decided yet," or, "If the couriers are American it will be because the exhibition is being indemnified by the U.S. Government," or some such nonsense. What I really want to say is, "Go practice on somebody else's exhibition." What I really want to say is, "Lay off me!" Two seconds later someone says, "We feel strongly that New Zealand packers should be used." And two seconds after that John says, "The museums are unhappy with the companies here and request that American packers be brought over."

They are wearing me down. This place is also very bad for my ego. No one knows what a registrar is and I am perceived as some kind of librarian or the one who does the paperwork. I no longer try very hard to explain. They don't always know what a conservator is either but they've got Cap figured because she is an archaeologist as well and they know what that is.

I had to stay home from work today because this damn sore

throat just won't quit! I can't believe it. There were only five objects left to do at the museum and Cap said she could finish without me. There I was for the first time on my own, but sick. I've been sorely tempted to hop in our little Austin Mini (Cap says it's like driving an egg beater, which is a completely apt description, I love it) and tootle off to do some sightseeing. Of course I haven't. I stayed in the hotel room and sipped tea and napped all day. I feel a bit better.

I must admit, my spirits have slipped back into the mire and I can't seem to get them out. These people are just wearing me down, that's all.

I'll write when I'm in better shape.

Love,

Carol

     *   *   *   *   *

During the night the wind reaches frightening levels. I sleep fitfully, aware of the rattling, thumping windows. Several times I roll over, certain that now, just now, the window is going to blow in. I want it to hit me in the back instead of the face. "It's a sou'wester," says the woman at the desk when we check out in the morning. "It finally came in during the night. Been due for days." I don't know quite what a sou'wester is, but I nod solemnly. I know it is something to be reckoned with.

We get to the ferry terminal at 7:00 to find that the sailing has been delayed indefinitely due to "adverse weather conditions in Cook Strait." Some people make sounds of displeasure but I am happy enough not to be out on the water just then. A man comes out of the office to change the signboard. "Conditions in Cook Strait," it says. He slides out the slate that says "rough" and slides in the one that says "very rough." I can see that these are the only two slates there are. My colleague and I check our bags and find an empty wooden bench. We prepare to wait.

At 10:15 boarding begins. There is a nurse greeting passengers as they enter. This makes me nervous. "Why is there a uniformed nurse on a ferry boat?" I wonder. I discuss with my colleague where to sit and decide on the bow where we will have a view in three directions. It has been said that there are beautiful things to see. At 10:40 the nurse comes up and forcefully suggests that we move midships. I am alarmed now. She is handing out white seasick bags. I think maybe I don't want to see the South Island that bad, but the ship has just pushed off from the dock. We are on our way.

The ferry begins to pitch forward and back almost immediately. I look out the porthole window next to me. One minute I can see only a wall of water, the next we are perched on top and I can see the retching sea.

I am terrified but not sick. I have always been afraid of the sea and now my heart has lodged in the back of my mouth. "Gee," my colleague says coolly, "we haven't even cleared the harbor yet." I am not encouraged. My lungs, liver and assorted other entrails move up to join my heart in the back of my mouth. It is crowded back there.

In twenty minutes the ship clears the harbor and sets off into open water. It begins to roll sideways at the same time that it is pitching forward and back. I have to look farther up now when I look out the porthole to see the top of the swells. I no longer feel afraid. I feel sick instead. My entrails move back down to approximately where they belong and something else takes their place in the back of my throat. I fight it for as long as I can. This is a three-and-a-half-hour crossing and there is a long way to go. For an hour I concentrate on breathing deeply and finally admit that I am losing ground.

I drag myself up and lurch across the cabin. At various times I find I am holding onto the back of a bench, the wall, or someone's head. It is hard to know which way I am going. When I reach the corridor it is easier because there is less room to lurch in and when I reach the bathroom I feel betrayed, disillusioned. It is lurching too. Certain places should be sanctuaries. I drag myself into the stall and contemplate which end of me to stick in the toilet. I sit. There is a horizontal bar on the inside of the door and I hold onto it with both hands, swaying violently with the ship. It reminds me of the time my cousin tried to teach me to water ski.

After some time it is clear that there is no point in continuing to sit here. I come out and lunge for the sink, splash water on my face and then watch my dripping face in the mirror. I make no attempt to wipe the water off even though it is running down my neck. I know only that I can't stand here staring into my own misery any longer.

I turn away from the sink and set my sights on the door, anticipating which way the ship will roll next. I take a step. When I get up off the floor I am back in the toilet stall. Wild hysterical laughter or thick tears are starting to close off my throat. Maybe both. In time I make my way back to my seat where my colleague has fallen asleep. I am furious at her for being able to do this. Furious at her smug shoulders, calm repose that grew up in Maine or somewhere on the sea where people know about boats. I lie down and try to remember if I've read that this is the thing to do or the thing not to do. I pray that now, just now, a steward will come through the ship asking who wants to be shot.

Some time goes by, some time roughly equivalent to the entire reign of a pope, and finally the sea seems slightly calmer.

I stand up now, slowly and with some dignity. I am going out on the deck. I have made this decision because I sense that I am finally going to throw up, or I am going to die, or I am going to throw up and then die, or I am going to die and then throw up. I doesn't seem to make any difference. I am going out on deck where there is air.

I am aware that I will probably be washed overboard and look forward to this eagerly. I step out the door prepared to scream obscenities at the nurse if she tries to stop me. I look like Joan of Arc. I wait for the wave and when it doesn't come I lean on the railing with my forearms and put my head in my hands. I begin to breathe; gasping, gulping, desperate breaths until the clean sea air fills my entire body. I lean forward so that I can vomit over the railing.

"You wouldn't be one of the American delegation, would you?" a man's voice says. I look up, incredulous, and find two men hanging onto the railing not far from me. I stare at them and begin to laugh. I laugh and laugh and laugh until the men think I have gone crazy and I know that I have. They begin to laugh with me.

The ship has reached Queen Charlotte Sound and the sea has become calm. I am going to live.

*　　　　*　　　　*　　　　*　　　　*

November 14, 1982, Nelson, N.Z.
The American Federation of Arts
New York, U.S.A.

Greetings,

I finally connected with Lesley in Nelson (remember my New Zealand friend whom I met in New York?). I had begun to lose hope of seeing her at all, but as we drove into Nelson, I knew she was there. I can't explain it. She and her husband Kevin have just moved back to New Zealand after eight years out of the country. They left New York only three days ahead of me and didn't know where they'd be living so she gave me phone numbers of friends and relatives whose couches they might be sleeping on. Every time we got into one of those towns I'd call, to find that they had either just left or had not yet arrived. Anyway, when I got to Nelson I called her in-laws and sure enough, she was sitting about five blocks away from our motel. She came over and we went to dinner, just the two of us since Kevin was up in Auckland house-hunting.

After dinner we sat around on the floor drinking wine and talking. She was the very first person I've been able to really talk to since leaving home. It was such a relief!

Today was about the worst I've gotten in terms of strung-out nerves. I just felt like crying all day. This evening was a shot in the arm that should last a long time.

I'm falling asleep from two glasses of cheap wine.

Love,

Carol

Lesley:

"Look, I just can't believe these things you're telling me!"

"Well, I'm not making them up. Don't laugh. They gave us all prayer books so we could pray and sing together and become one family."

"Was this only here in Nelson?"

"No, no. I mean, the ceremonies have varied a lot from place to place and we aren't always lucky enough to get prayer books and all, but this has gone on in every town so far except Auckland."

"Why not Auckland? No ancestors in Auckland?"

"Actually, I'm finding out that some Maoris are a little annoyed at Auckland for not having a ceremony. We just walked right in and started handling objects. It was our first stop, so nothing seemed odd about that to me."

"I guess they've gotten a little too 'white' about things in Auckland."

"Mmmm. That's the point, I gather. A minister came and took us to tea the first day and it only dawned on me recently—that was their token effort at a ceremony. But by then we'd already handled a quarter of the objects."

"Oops! Better watch out then."

"We're being awful, you know. Do you think I'll be struck by lightning?"

"Of course you will."

Lesley later on:

"This is amazing!"

"Look, why are you so surprised? You grew up here. You both grew up here. These things I'm telling you shouldn't be new."

"Well they are, I tell you. I'm shocked that my friend has to come from New York to tell me about it. Oh, there were some Maoris in school with us and all, but we never had that much to do with them."

"I'm glad I dropped by to educate you."

"So do you believe all this stuff?"

"Look, I can't say I believe it, but I sure as hell know that they do. I grew up Catholic, twelve years of Catholic school. That never really did much for me either, let me tell you. I know some Catholics though, who would fight you to the death if you tried to tell them that little round white thing is not the body of Christ, and that cheap red wine is not his blood. So aren't we smart and sophisticated?"

"You're right. You're absolutely right. I guess everybody's got their beliefs."

"Right. So if I need to be cleared with the ancestors before I can handle the objects, that's fine with me. In fact, the point is that as far as the Maori people are concerned, these are not objects at all. They *are* their ancestors."

"I guess you're right to just go along with what they believe in."

November 15, 1982, Nelson, N.Z.
The American Federation of Arts
New York, U.S.A.

Dear everyone,

Time for a work update. Our system now has all the bugs worked out of it and is going reasonably well with me finding and identifying, Cap inspecting and John photographing. Amazingly enough, the time schedule Cap and I made up in New York based on the numbers of objects and their sizes has worked out. Where we planned one day, we've needed one and where we planned five days, we've needed five. What is a little hair-raising is that we didn't anticipate the ceremonies. They take up a good part of the first day, which is not so bad if we are going to be at that museum for two days or more. It is a near disaster when we have only the day, or worse, half a day. This is the case most of the time and we spend much of the ceremony and the tea that follows trying not to look at our watches. I tried to see if we could dispense with all the tea and cookies in the interest of time but found that the sharing of food is an integral part of the ceremony itself and cannot be dispensed with.

At the same time I have collected masses of information to be used later in planning the assembly and packing. Most of it is frightening. There are apparently no art packers as we know them in New Zealand. There are no air-ride vans. Since none of these objects have ever left the museums in which they currently live, almost no one has any idea how to pack them for temporary transport to a central consolidation point. They don't have or know where to get packing material. On and on. I've checked into lumber yards and I think we can get all the supplies we need on that front, but possibly not the foam rubber or the flannel and maybe some of the hardware. I may have to ship that down from New York when it's time. It has also been interesting driving all over the country and knowing that these are exactly the routes that trucks will have to take when they are carrying the artifacts to the packing site. The ancestors are going to have to take that damn ferry too! I have not yet found a packing site. The National Museum in Wellington is the only possibility so far and is a pretty grim one in terms of space and equipment.

Our greeting ceremony in Nelson was like a scene from a Fellini movie. Cap and I picked up Peta and John at the airport and the four of us raced to the museum for a 10:00 ceremony. The museum is a one-storey, concrete building that looks just like where I went to first grade. We parked along the side of the building and Peta told us to wait there by the car while he let them know we had arrived. What seems to be going on here, what I've gathered from all the ceremonies so far, is that we, the visitors, need to be "called in" by the Maori/museum hosts. Peta came back, said they were ready and led us slowly around the corner of the building. Sure enough, there was the now familiar off-key wail from the front steps. There were four or five Maoris and the museum director. He wore a sweater and corduroys. The wailing woman wore a bright blue polyester doubleknit dress with snagged threads all over it. She wore thick-soled heavy shoes and to pull the whole outfit together, a kiwi feather cloak that came to her knees. The wispy grey feathers matched her hair. There were several men whose suits perfectly complemented her dress. One of them also wore a feather cloak.

Peta led us to the four chairs on the other side of the narrow gravel driveway and motioned us to sit. There was a lovely garden on this side of the building and there must have been sheep somewhere nearby but unseen. We could hear them making sheep noises while pigeons burbled around the legs of our chairs.

There was a series of formal speeches in Maori and English and some way into this, the sound of a distant motor grew louder and louder. Suddenly a small motorbike appeared around the corner of the museum. The bike was being driven by a middle-aged Maori man wearing shorts and one artificial leg. He puttered quietly up the driveway, looking neither to the left nor the right as he passed through the narrow space separating our chairs from the speech-making Maoris on the museum steps.

There was nothing, in expression or voice, to indicate that anyone had seen this vision at all. Not a beat was missed. When the speeches were done we were each handed prayer books so that we might pray and sing together, thereby becoming one family. The most horrible, unsynchronized, gravelly singing imaginable ensued, and finally the ceremony was done.

A battered wooden table was carried from the museum and covered with white paper which they taped to its edges. Tea was brought out and two bags of chocolate chip cookies were torn open. It was at this point that the sound of a distant motor grew louder and louder. Suddenly the motorbike appeared from the other side of the building. The one-legged man in shorts looked neither to the right nor the left as he rode through the narrow space separating us from two bags of chocolate chip cookies. When he had disappeared we were each handed a cup of tea and people began to ask us questions about the exhibition.

I don't know, guys. I just don't know. We're off to Christchurch now.

Love to everyone,
Carol

The hotel clerk:

"Excuse me, was that you I saw on the front page today?"

"Yes, it was. I think we've been on the front page of every newspaper in New Zealand by now."

Cap:

"Here's another one!"

"Yes, I think I've now been misquoted by every newspaper in New Zealand. Did you see this?"

"They do have a way of twisting things around, don't they?"

"I'm not talking to anyone else who has a tape recorder. In fact, if they have a pencil in their hand I won't talk to them either. I'm obviously far to naive for this."

November 16, 1982, Christchurch, N.Z.
The American Federation of Arts
New York, U.S.A.

Hi everyone,

We have now arrived in Christchurch and will soon go track down some dinner. Tomorrow morning we are due at the museum here for our ceremony. It was quite entertaining, this little jaunt from Nelson to Christchurch. We checked out our maps and decided we had time, for once, to take what appeared to be the more scenic route. It was scenic all right. At a certain point the road went from standard, paved, one lane in each direction, to unpaved. Not long after that the road became somewhat narrow and a bit winding. Not long after that we were climbing so steeply that our little rental car was at a crawl in first gear. By that time the road was only a little over one car's width across. We wondered what we might do if a car came from the other direction. There was no need to worry. No one else was stupid enough to have taken this road. We crawled up and down the most alarmingly steep and rutted roads for about an hour and then saw a small sign that read, "Watercourse #1." "Gee," we all said, "I wonder what that could mean?"

What it meant was that around the next hairpin turn there was a goddamned stream across the road. We just looked at each other and started to laugh. John was driving at that point so he just shrugged and rolled cautiously through it. It wasn't very deep. A little further along, on a very steep climb, a good bit of the road was washed out. That was seriously frightening as it looked like a sure bet that the rest of the road would soon follow. When we got to the sign for Watercourse #2 we started to giggle immediately. This one was deeper and had more large rocks in it. By this time Cap was driving and took it calmly but cautiously. Watercourse #3 was deeper yet and we were starting to worry about how many more there might be since they were definitely increasing in all dimensions as well as in force. We got a little quiet. We were anticipating the Mississippi around the next bend. #4 was a fright. I got out and took a picture of the car about to ford, then rolled up my pants and went out to the middle to see how deep it really was. It was forceful enough to almost drag me along to where it crashed over an embankment. We got through, but it was scary.

About a half hour later there was a flock of sheep sound asleep in the road. They woke and looked up but didn't seem terribly concerned about the red thing coming at them. They probably hadn't seen too many of them on this particular road. I got out and made them move.

I am starving. More later.

Love,

Carol

*   *   *   *   *

The museum is smaller than some and larger than others. It is made of grey stone. I wait patiently with my colleagues in a hallway just inside the door. In time I hear the call. I hear the odd, eerie wail that wobbles slightly as it rises to an off-key crescendo and then begins to fall gradually away. My feet begin to move, slowly shuffling beside my colleagues and the wail continues to electrify the air until we are all inside the room. It follows us to our chairs and on its last breath there is the boom of other voices with other kinds of power. Then there is silence. Crashing silence.

Out of the silence a voice begins to speak. The voice is a man's voice and he moves forward among his people. He speaks at some length in this language that is foreign and musical and has many hard edges. I do not understand any of it but I am intrigued by its strangeness. When the man is done a second man stands up and begins to speak. He speaks in the same odd language and at different times seems angry or impassioned. He speaks violently and waves his arms. Soon he speaks in my own language but by the time the third man stands my attention has begun to wander. The speeches are familiar and there is no need to pay attention. I will not be called on to respond because I am a woman. Even though it is to me that they speak it is someone else sitting to my left who will answer for me. He is a man.

Instead of listening I begin to inspect these people. They are brown. Some more than others. Some are in their middle years and most older. All are a little too wide. Most wear ill-fitting clothes. There is one more speech and then the man to my left stands up and begins to speak to them in their mutual language. He is young and looks more Italian than I do. I trust that he is responding well for me because I have heard him speak in English and can only hope to be as eloquent.

He finishes and there are songs and prayers and then we are all led to another room where there is tea and pink cakes.

Now we are led again through intricate corridors and down a flight of stairs. The man who leads is tall and has some authority here. He takes us to a room that is long and narrow and artificially lit. Down the center there is a long, wide counter and on the counter there are sixteen things. The things are nearly all wooden though some are bone or stone and some ivory. They are pendants, canoe prows and carvings of ancestors. Some are large and some very small. I have seen only poor photographs of these things and now I can see that they are all very beautiful or at least simple and elegant.

I begin to watch the brown people because they don't know what to do. The women stand awkwardly and clutch their white pocketbooks. The men shuffle a little from foot to foot. The fiery speeches and powerful wails are done now and here, in this clinical room with chrome sinks, they do not know what to do. The tall man speaks because he can see that it is his role to do that. He encourages everyone to look at the objects and then goes on to caution us. "They are very fragile," he says, "and must be handled with extreme care and held only by their strongest points and only over the counter." I listen to his long list of cautions. I have heard this speech before. I have made this speech before. It is a formal speech, a museum speech. The man finishes and waits expectantly as if something ought to happen. Nothing happens. I laugh out loud and everyone turns to me. I shift my body, soften it, make it casual. "Notice," I say, "how everyone backs away from the table after that speech." I am careful to keep a grin on my face. The tall man blushes but laughs with me and says no, really, it is all right to touch them, and then everything is okay and the people begin to move.

They are tentative at first, but then more and more excited.

Some time goes by and discussions are had about the origins of this and the uses of that. They point and laugh and pick up the things made by their ancestors. They look and look with joy and wonder in their faces. They look in a way I have not seen faces look before and something strange begins to crawl in my body.

Soon they seem satisfied and there is another pause, another silence. Out of the silence a voice begins to speak. The voice is a man's and starts very low. He steps forward a little and everyone tries to hear what he is saying. He says it again, not louder, still in a whisper, but with more certainty this time. "I am afraid," he says. The man is beautiful. A beautiful brown man with white hair like down and hands that are massive but not thick. He is not tall and his trousers were made for someone tall so that they crumple, in front, over his worn shoes. He speaks gently, twisting a button on his brown cardigan and in the small, close room, no one moves.

"I'm afraid they won't come back," he says. His voice is hoarse. He smiles at me in apology and in his eyes I see anguish. "Something like that," he says and nods his head towards a small wooden comb interwoven with linen threads, "something like that might not ever come back." His voice breaks a little and I can see that there are tears making their way down his brown cheeks. He reaches out with one hand and touches the comb, and the thing that was crawling in my body crawls up my back and down my arms and my palms begin to sweat. I am horrified now by something I cannot name and I stare from his face to his hand. Suddenly I know that what I have just seen was not a touch at all but a caress and for one very brief second I see but not with my eyes. Then I know but not with my mind and I think I will weep. My spokesman steps forward now.

He speaks quietly of their fears and nods to me indicating that I should begin my speech. My mind screams. It screams, no, this is not what is wanted here. It is not what is needed, but I speak anyway. I tell them about couriers and trucks with air-ride suspension. I tell them about foam rubber and cotton flannel and climate control. I tell them that I will personally supervise the packing of the objects. I show them glossy photographs of the packing system. I explain that I will personally escort the objects to New York, that I will unpack and inspect them in New York. I explain that I will do this at the beginning and end of each and every stop on the tour. Then I turn and say, "Besides." I look right at the beautiful brown man and point at him, my arm outstretched. "Besides," I say again, staring into his face, "I will be thinking of you every *second* that I am with these things." The man grabs my pointing finger and then my whole hand. He pulls me forward and embraces me so hard I cannot breathe and then he pushes me back. He holds my arms and looks into my eyes. "Thank you," he says very softly and kisses my cheek. "You're welcome," I say very softly, and for a moment he knows that I know.

Then it is over and the room starts to move. The brown people say how pleased they are to have met us and wish us well. They file out of the room and I am left with my colleagues to go about my work. Soon I am absorbed with my cameras and tape measures and papers and soon I have forgotten. I remember only that a beautiful brown man in Christchurch has asked a favor of me. I remember that I said yes.

*   *   *   *   *

November 15, 1982, Christchurch, N.Z.

Jamie Summers
New York, U.S.A.

Dear Jamie,

Something truly amazing has happened that is very hard to explain. I had a brief interaction with one of the elders this morning that has completely changed my way of thinking about the exhibition and about these incredible people. It has also, strangely, made me very sad and frightened about what we are about to do. I'm not so sure any more that I'm proud of my role in taking these objects out of the country. There was a confusing moment this morning when I seem to have stepped out of the room, out of the circumstances somehow, and seen how things *really* are with these people.

My mind is going a little crazy, thinking back over all the Maori people I've met since I got here. Is this man different? Is he special or were they all like this? Was I different three weeks ago or have I just not been paying attention? I just don't know anymore. As I said, I'm very sad and very scared and can't explain it.

    Love,
    Carol

                                  November 21, 1982, Dunedin, N.Z.
The American Federation of Arts
New York, U.S.A.

Dear friends and colleagues!

On Friday this whole thing got funny. Yes, it finally became so awful that a certain element of comedy has begun to seep in and now at least I can laugh while my face is all broken out from nerves. (I'll be charging AFA for the Clearasil.)

We came roaring down to Dunedin from Christchurch—about a four-hour drive—to be at the museum by 3:00 P.M. for our welcoming ceremony. There were lots of Maoris waiting for us, not just the usual small group of elders. This time there were lots of young people as well with all their screaming children. "Gee, look at all these people," I stupidly thought. "What could they all be doing here?"

They invited us to come to their marae (meeting house) on the outskirts of town. They said we would be more formally welcomed there in conjunction with the greeting of a group from the Maori Women's Welfare League that was due to arrive then. As a result, the ceremony at the museum was very rushed. The children never stopped screaming and running all over the place.

After the ceremony, one of the men asked why there were no

men with us and then asked what I would do if there were a fire and everything burned up. Two nice, lightweight questions, don't you think? I ignored the one about the men because I am tired of trying to answer that and said it would of course be a tragedy if there were to be a fire. I then explained the US indemnity policy. Turns out I'd walked right into his trap. "Ha!" he says. "But how could money replace that?!" He points to the carved meeting house we are passing on our way to the boardroom where tea is to be served. Are you getting the picture that things were off to a very good start?

Once in the boardroom we found out why all the extra people were there. It was a bloody protest demonstration against the nasty Americans come to take their taonga (treasures) away. We'd been given a spokesman, some guy named Martin we hardly had time to meet. One of the elders stood up after the tea was poured and said the young people were there because they had something they wanted to say to Martin. (Unfortunately Peta could not be with us in Dunedin and Martin truly was regarded as our spokesman.) The museum director and curator, who had apparently known all about this and led us right into it without a word of warning, sat there and avoided my eyes while these university students proceeded to pour their hearts out. It was like being back in the Vietnam days at home.

They were actually very eloquent. They spoke about their anger and their fear. They talked about how much has been taken away from their people and how suspicious they are of anyone who wants to take more. They said they were not pleased by our presence and they were not pleased that their taonga were being taken away to be put in a "zoo" and stared at by people who didn't understand them. Their voices were shaking as they said all these things and I'll tell you, I was starting to shake too. I was getting angrier and angrier at having been put in this position. They addressed all this to Martin even though until then he had nothing to do with the exhibition. So of course, when they're done he gets up while I'm contemplating leaping to my feet. I was so angry by then I was willing to deal with the consequences of a woman speaking in front of the elders, who were sitting there watching.

Martin unfortunately proceeded to condescend to them in the most appalling, though I'm sure well-meaning, way. There, there, he says. This exhibition will be good for you because it will make you more aware of your heritage. More aware of their heritage!? They've just finished ripping their hearts out over tea and this will make them more aware of their heritage? Then he says how much more qualified the Americans are to take care of their taonga because we have men with big guns in our museums to guard them. By this time I was apoplectic. You have to understand that as far as they are concerned, this man was expressing my thoughts, our thoughts. Aren't you pleased? I bet you didn't know you had such noble thoughts.

I was so angry by then I did leap to my feet. I figured it just couldn't get worse. It just couldn't. I thanked Martin but said that I didn't think a New Zealander could speak for what was in the mind of an American, just as I didn't feel that I could speak for a New Zealander. I turned to the elders and apologized for violating their traditions but said I felt it was very important that I speak for myself. They didn't say anything. Everyone was a little white by then. I felt like death and was shaking so hard I had to hold onto the edge of the table to keep from sinking back to the floor.

I swear I didn't know what was going to come out of my mouth. I could hardly figure why I'd stood up to begin with. I just started to talk. I said that I too felt anger. I said that I felt anger because we were being attacked when no one had bothered to find out why we were there. I said that we were technicians, there to do a job and that we would do it well; that we had no more influence over whether the exhibition went than they did. I told them that all that had happened seven years ago, and if they were unhappy they should have been on their museum director's doorstep protesting seven years ago. They should have been in Wellington seven years ago, protesting to their own government who suggested the whole thing to begin with. I said that I could now explain how carefully we would handle the objects throughout the tour, but that if I did it would feel as if I were defending myself. I said I didn't feel I needed to defend myself to them.

At the end I said that perhaps I agreed with them, but that it hardly mattered anymore. I told them they now had my anger to mix with their own.

Well, they understood. They filed out one at a time and shook my hand as they went. They asked if I could see that their message got to the proper people and I promised that I would do that. Then the elders stood. One of the women came up to me and took my hand. "I feel sorry for you," she said. "You have a tremendous responsibility." They all left. I almost started to sob as we were whisked into cars and raced out to the marae for the "more official" welcome. Under the circumstances I wanted to refuse to go but couldn't get it together fast enough.

Round two was no improvement. After a long, lovely greeting to the Women's Welfare League, the guy with the fire question stood up. "And greetings to you," he said, gesturing in our general direction in the crowd (about 75 people were there), "welcome to you—I've forgotten your names—but welcome to you who have come to take our taonga away. I said to one of the girls at the museum, one of these girls they send to do men's work, I said what if there's a fire and it all burns up and she said, oh it was insured for a lot of money. But can money replace our taonga? No! But anyway, welcome to you." He waved rudely and sat down.

You guessed it. Martin started to stand up and I lunged for his arm but he stood up anyway. He made the same basic speech only this time it seemed worse because he took what I had said at the museum and twisted it around just enough so that it came out sounding like an excuse, like blaming it all on someone else. Hey, we're just the flunkies they sent down to do this. We don't know nothing. You know, that kind of thing. My composure was slipping away. He sat down and John, sitting next to me, said "She'll be right. It's all fine now. Just leave it alone." "It's not all fine," I said. "It's not all fine and I must speak to them." I tried to get up but Cap restrained me. I didn't see it then, but she was right. I'd gotten away with it at the museum because they were all a little out of their element, but here? Christ only knows what would have happened if I'd stood up and opened my mouth.

Then there was an enormous receiving line and all the nose bumping. We just stood by our chairs. Cap and I agreed that we should probably leave, but we couldn't think of how to affect that. After a while someone grabbed us and pushed us into the line. "This welcome is for you too," they said. "I've never felt less welcome in my life," I said back. Some of the elders nearby looked very embarrassed by all this. A research doctor from the university came up to me then. I was pretty clear at that point that he had been the spearhead of the whole thing even though he'd been kindly shepherding us around all day. "I hope you aren't too culture-shocked by the day's events," he said sweetly. Under cover of the noise of pots and pans and tables being set up for the meal I screamed at him. I said I *was* shocked. I said I agreed with the students and that I also took exception to being brought somewhere on the pretence of being greeted and then being harangued in public in an arena where I could not defend myself. That was the first time he seemed to get it from my point of view. Then he asked sweetly if we wanted a tour guide for the weekend.

Peta, on hearing this on the phone, was appalled. He said what we'd been through actually amounted to no more than bad manners and said all he could do was apologize for some ignorant Maoris. He is, in any case, flying down here to make sure it is not the elders themselves who have expressed displeasure with the exhibition.

Please send Valium. Love and kisses,
Carol

November 22, 1982, Dunedin, N.Z.
The American Federation of Arts
New York, U.S.A.

Hi folks,

My nose is getting sore. You see, every time we have a ceremony we have to bump noses, twice, with all the Maoris and museum personnel present. Usually there are only six or seven elders and one or two staff members, but on occasion there have been up to thirty people there. That takes quite a while after the greeting song and by the time you're through, it's about time for the farewell song and then you're in for another sixty nose bumps. What it comes down to is that you spend most of the time singing and bumping.

After a while I got pretty good at it and could bump right along there without cracking foreheads with anyone. In the beginning there is a tendency to close your eyes as you're coming in for a landing, but this is dangerous. You could miss and end up with your nose in someone's eye or some other place you wish it weren't. I must admit, there have been a few noses I would have preferred not to be become quite so intimate with, but I think it is considered bad form to discriminate about nose bumping.

All is quiet on the western and eastern fronts. But tomorrow we head south. Anyway, our day of work at the Otago Museum was uneventful in spite of our rocky entry into town on Friday. It seems the elders are quite embarrassed by what went on and are still in favor of the exhibition. Thank God Cap stopped me from trying to get up and speak on the marae, it would have been a terrible mistake.

We've now been here three weeks and it feels like three years. I've written a total of seventeen letters and twenty-two post-cards, in addition to writing in my journal nearly every night. It's what's keeping me sane in addition to being able to call Peta. It is true, however, that Friday pushed things onto an entirely new plane. It is all quite funny now and I can't wait to see what we run up against next.

The country is, without doubt, one of the most beautiful places on earth, however. You get bored with the beauty. Ho hum. One more staggering vista, one more breathtaking view of the sea. I've almost stopped taking pictures because I've lost my ability to discriminate. You could easily stop every fifteen feet and snap another as the view gets better and better around every curve in the road.

'Bye for now,
Carol

Lesley:

"A protest demonstration!? You're joking! Where?"

"Dunedin. We were met by a group of foaming-at-the-mouth Maoris who were not thrilled with the nasty Americans come to take their sacred ancestors away."

"Good God! In quiet little Dunedin!"

"Quiet little Dunedin with a university full of militant Maoris."

A Maori elder:

"I understand you're here to take our taonga to America."

"No, no. I'm just here to look at them . . . just to look."

Cap:

"This is not a lot of fun."

"You're not kidding. What do you think is going to happen when I *do* come back to try to walk out of the country with these?"

"I really can't imagine."

Lesley:

"Look, why are you people putting on this bloody show if nobody wants it to go? You're killing yourself."

"Hey, it wasn't my idea. I actually used to think it was a pretty neat idea but I've come to some different thinking about it. Besides, it's not everyone who doesn't want the things to go. In some cases the museums that own the stuff say yes and the local Maoris say no. In other cases, it's the other way around. It's just very controversial, that's all."

"Controversial is being a little mild, don't you think?"

"Maybe so. None of the stuff has ever been out of New Zealand before. The other day I was told by a curator at the museum in Dunedin that every disaster, every earthquake, every kid that gets hit by a school bus is going to be blamed on these objects being off New Zealand soil. Not too heavy, huh?"

"Oh, this is nice. Very nice. You can't say you lead a boring life!"

Cap:

"You should try not to let it bother you."

"It's all he says! 'She'll be right, mate. She'll be right.' Well, as a matter of fact, she *won't* be right. As a matter of fact, people are chasing us with big sticks and she won't be right!"

"It can be quite irritating."

"Irritating? If John says that one more time I'll kill him!"

November 25, 1982, Queenstown, N.Z.
The American Federation of Arts
New York, U.S.A.

Happy Non-Thanksgiving,

We are sitting in our worst cinder-block motel yet. The bathroom is so small you can sit on the toilet and brush your teeth at the same time. It is cold enough that I have the hood up on my sweatshirt as I sit here writing. I look like a leprechaun. It is also pissing down rain outside.

Observation #1: They have not yet invented food in New Zealand. We stopped for lunch at what was one of the two eating establishments for seventy-five miles. We chose what appeared to be scrambled eggs and cheese on a roll and turned out to be canned, creamed corn on hamburger buns. Another classic favorite on all the menus is spaghetti on toast. (That's canned spaghetti on white bread toast.) I've been avoiding this like the plague as I suspect it can cause instant heart failure in anyone of Italian descent.

Observation #2: We have recently been to Pupu Springs, Pipi Scenic Reserve and Kaka Creek. I leave you to draw your own conclusions.

Observation #3: Sheep are very, very stupid animals. Every time you round a bend in the road and find a few sheep in the middle of it (often), they begin to run down the road in front of the car. Mom and her sheeplets clattering smack down the middle of the white line if there is one. It never occurs to them to veer off to the side! They just try to outrun the monster behind them in a total panic. The only thing to do is to gradually gain on them and nudge them off the road.

The cows are even worse. When you round the bend and come upon a bunch of cows they try to walk through the car as if they don't see it. It is a red car. It is very hard not to see. Then they drool all over the car. The best thing to do when you suddenly find yourself in the middle of a herd of cows is to close the windows. That eliminates the possibility of getting a lap full of cow spit. Next you turn off the car and take a nap or read a good book while they figure out they're supposed to go *around* you.

In all seriousness, we are actually having some fun at the moment. (Yes, it's true!) We finished work at the museum in Invercargill on Wednesday evening and don't have to be anywhere until Monday morning when we're expected at the Taranaki Museum in New Plymouth, back on the North Island. John has gone off for good because he has another commitment and . . . well, we are free! Four whole days!

We'd been reading some guidebooks in anticipation of this potential break and knew that the west coast of the South Island is supposed to have the most spectacular scenery in New Zealand. Everyone said we couldn't possibly drive from Invercargill up to the Picton ferry with a stop at Milford Sound in four days. I guess they don't know any New York drivers. We decided that we were unwilling to simply fly over all the greatest country.

We're going to make it. We drove all the way into Milford Sound yesterday, which was fabulous and eerie. The only drawback is that this part of the country gets approximately 250 inches of rainfall a year, and about 200 of them have fallen on us in the last two days. No matter, it is beautiful even in the rain.

One more note about work that you should all enjoy. I went to one of the Management Committee meetings while in Wellington. At that meeting it came out that the exhibition will have to open according to Maori custom, with two ceremonies at dawn.

There sat fifteen people from the Department of Maori Affairs, the Department of Internal Affairs, the Queen Elizabeth II Arts Council, the Maori Council and the Anglican Church. There sat all these people looking at me for a reaction. I didn't even throw up on the conference table. Aren't you proud of me? (I did gag a bit.) I told them I was not the one to properly address the issue, but that if two ceremonies at dawn are required they should inform AFA immediately. I mentioned that the Met is not in the habit of holding ceremonies at dawn every other Tuesday morning and that it might take some special arranging. Peta plans to discuss it with all of you when he's there. Have fun.

I feel as if I've been transported to another planet. All the cars, telephones, airplanes and business suits are obviously a trick to deceive me into thinking this is 1982 on planet Earth.

Love,
Carol

P.S. Speaking of phones, some of these towns have three-digit phone numbers! Also, we climbed on Franz Josef Glacier yesterday. Spectacular! I've got a lot of great slides to show when I get home.

*   *   *   *   *

This is about driving. I put the pedal to the floor and I do not wait for highways. If I were to wait for highways I would wait my whole life. "Metal surface," the sign says, and I begin to wonder what this means when abruptly the pavement ends and stones begin to batter themselves against the bottom of the car. "I think it means gravel road," I say to myself and hit the brake to slow down before flinging rock breaks our windshield or someone else's.

I drive with both hands on the wheel, arms straight and drive fiercely all the time. Once off the gravel I push it back up, 50, 55, 70 miles an hour. There is a slow car in front of us now. I pin myself to his bumper, I tail him, darting in and out, in and out, waiting for a break. Then there is a break and I fly out to the right and around and he is gone.

"One lane bridge," the sign says. "Please give way." I do not slow down until the bridge is in sight and then I pull back slightly. I assess the situation and when it is clear that there are no cars coming from the other direction, when it is clear that the bridge is mine, I sweep across it, 25, 40, 45 miles an hour, whatever its narrowness will bear. We are off the bridge and my left hand finds the shift, pushing it back up through the gears.

The curves I take with style. I use both lanes, the one that is mine and the one that is not. I drift back and forth between them to soften the curves, but am wary and tensed at all times for sheep, dogs, cars in the road. Anything might be on the road. Trees down on the road, geese on the road, anything. "One lane bridge," the sign says again and I see that this is a long one.

When we draw closer I see also that we will share this bridge not only with cars coming from the other side, but with a train. When I am sure that all is clear I dive onto the bridge and fly across it, this time faster than its narrowness will bear, terrified that one or the other, the car or the train, will loom into view finding us only halfway across. The train tracks catch at the tyres, dragging us into the gully, so I run the rest of the way in the gully because I cannot break out.

Up the hills and around snarled curves it is agony. I drop back to third gear, second, even first. The car crawls and I think I will scream and suddenly we are over the rise and get to come down. I swoop and dip and lean into the curves and all around us mountains fly by. Green hills, craggy peaks, rocky coastline dance at the corners of my eyes. I keep my eyes on the white line.

Can we make Te Anau by 1:00? Queenstown by nightfall? Hokitika by noon? "It's still 104 miles to Westport," says the navigator, atlas in lap. "I think we can do it," I say, and concentrate harder on the curves. I chide myself for taking that one too loosely, swinging too wide and on the next I pull it in tight and am pleased. "There's a beautiful view!" comes the shout, and I hit the shoulder. The gravel flies and when the car has almost stopped I pull the parking brake, the car lurches to a halt. Our hands reach around and find cameras just behind the seat while the other hands have already opened the doors. We both jump out. The shutters click, one, two, maybe three shots and the gravel flies again. We are back on the road.

Now we come down off the mountain and ahead is straight road. I release a long breath and for just a moment I send my eyes on vacation. They stray, briefly, over the turquoise sea and towering rocks. Then I pull them back in and put the pedal to the floor.

*   *   *   *   *

November 29, 1982, New Plymouth, N.Z.
The American Federation of Arts
New York, U.S.A.

Witch Trials at Taranaki.

Two American women were found guilty of witchcraft by a tribunal of twenty Maoris here today. Their heads were shaved and they were burned at the stake in the central hall of the Taranaki Museum in New Plymouth. As the flames leapt towards the ceiling, one of the women was heard to yell,

"Douglas Newton, you die for this!" followed by, "I want a raise!"

Only kidding, guys. Here's what really happened at Taranaki. We arrived in New Plymouth and were met at the airport by Gavin Johnson, the conservator who is John's replacement. We were quite green from a horrible flight. When we got to the museum we were greeted at the door by a Maori Mafia Don (three-piece suit, silver-tipped cane, heavy gold rings, etc.) and his gun moll. "Ah, it is good to see you," he says. "There are many people waiting. I hope our outcome will be favorable."

Outcome? I thought. What outcome? Are we having a trial? I began to eye the hideous blue station wagon thinking there might still be time for an escape. It was too late. He already had his arm around my shoulder and was heading me for the museum door. His gun moll brought up the rear, shepherding Cap and poor innocent Gavin behind.

"Yes," says the Don, named Tommy, "there is much concern here and many questions. Harsh words may be spoken but don't worry, I'll be with you. By the end of our meeting today perhaps we will have a good answer. I warn you though," he went on, "the outcome depends on our eloquence." Eloquence? What eloquence? Whose eloquence? The hell with eloquence, I want out of here! But by that time the greeting call could be heard from inside and he had jettisoned us through the door.

We got through the ceremony, the prayers, the formal speeches in Maori and English and the tea and cookies and then they set up the chairs. Five together for me, Cap, Gavin, Tommy and his friend, and about twenty facing us. These quickly filled with Maoris, both old and young. My palms were beginning to sweat and I grabbed Tommy aside. "Look," I said, "you've got the wrong person. I need to explain something to you about . . ." "No," he says. "You need to explain it to them," and he points to the twenty grim and expectant faces. "They have come to see you, to look at you, to hear you and to make their opinions. They have come to answer their fears." Then the fun began.

Have you ever watched four or five seagulls when they find a piece of meat on the beach? Well, for an appetizer we had, "Can you tell us something about the museums where the exhibition would go if it did take place?" (Tommy whispers in my ear, "Tell them about King Tut. They'll want to hear that.") Followed by, "If Mobil Oil has any involvement in this, we feel strongly that they must get no publicity because they are drilling holes all over our town and destroying our seafood resources." At some point early on I managed to explain that we were technicians and that while I would try to answer their questions, there would be many I could not answer. "Ah, yes," they all murmured, and kept pecking at the piece of meat. For a main course we had, "Why have they sent women to do this work? How do we know someone will not make replicas of our artifacts and send us back the fakes?" and "Who is making all the money from this exhibition?" For dessert there was a truly heartrending speech about how the Maori taonga is alive, not dead chunks of wood, and how they do not, like the rest of the world, separate the artifacts from the people. They are one and the same.

I did my best, guys. I tell you, I did my best. I contemplated just saying that I was not the appropriate person to address these issues but as Tommy said, they had come to make judgments. I figured they would make them based on what I said or based on my failure to say anything.

"Now," says their leader when I had finished, "now we will have a vote. If it is nay, you will not have to look at the artifacts at all." It was 2:00 P.M. We'd been up since 6:30 to catch an early flight, the flight was a horror, we'd had no breakfast and no lunch and had not seen a bathroom since dawn. My corpse was picked to shreds and I wanted nothing more than to hear them say "nay" and run out of there. I knew, however, that we were not leaving without doing what we had come to do. I knew, somewhere in the back of my muddled brain, that even if they voted nay this would not be the final word, that it would be "appealed," so to speak. I knew also that if that were to happen

I could not come skipping back to New Zealand next month to see the fifteen artifacts I hadn't seen. So I made one last speech. I asked them to please listen to me carefully before they took a vote. Christ knows what I said. I just don't know anymore what it was that I said but at the end I told them there was no need for them to reach a decision today. I said if they decided not to lend, the papers could always be thrown away, but that we absolutely had to inspect the artifacts today. But no, they wanted to vote anyway, and wonder of wonders, we got a somewhat feeble "yes." "They feel good about you," Tommy whispers in my ear. Gee, ain't that nice . . .

Now what I really want to know, I mean what it is critical that I know is, how the *hell* (said with feeling) is it possible that no one knew this was going on? How the hell is it possible that I came down here thinking that all loans were secured and that I would be able to devote myself to the already colossal logistical requirements of this fiasco? Let me tell you guys, we don't need a registrar down here. We need the goddamned marines. All of them. Call in the National Guard, too.

And by the way, what are you supposed to say when some dragon lady in Wellington puts her hands on her hips and says in a how-do-you-like-that voice, "Well, Taranaki probably won't lend at all, and then the rest of the museums will withdraw anything from the Taranaki region as a gesture of support and that will knock out 25% of your show." I mean really, what are you supposed to say to that? "Golly, gee . whiz, Sally, that's really nice and while you're at it, why don't you take that 25% of the show and cram it . . ." Would something like that be okay?

The Mafia Don carried a carved walking stick seven hundred years old that has been handed down through his family. He said it *is* his ancestor so-and-so, whose name, of course, I can neither pronounce nor remember. He takes "him" to bed with him every night and has managed, he says, to have twelve children in thirty or so years of marriage in spite of the extra party in the bed. I was waiting for him to pour it a cup of tea and feed it a cookie. Be seriously warned that anyone who says, on my return, "You should have said," or, "You could have done," will meet with massive amounts of hostility. I dare anyone sitting on Madison Avenue and 65th Street to recommend what I should have said to a middle-aged man in a business suit feeding tea and cookies to his walking stick!

By the time you read this I will be nearly in Australia, where I plan to hold my act together long enough to visit art packers in Sydney and Canberra. I then plan to lead as debauched a life as possible visiting my friend Margot whom I have not seen in seven years. Our reunion should be even more wonderful than it might have been before I lived through this six-week nightmare.

Perhaps I can return somewhat sounder of mind than I am right now and begin sifting through all the information gathered here.

I'm going off to have dinner with my left boot now. He has been handed down through my family for many years and he feels like having steak tonight.

Love,
Carol

P.S. I called Peta (who has the most extraordinary ability to not be around when disaster strikes). He was horrified but maintains that everything is just fine. You could have fooled me.

*   *   *   *   *

Lesley:

"What about that story you were going to tell me?"

"Oh, right. We were in Hamilton last week, at the Waikato Art Museum. I was taking all the condition photos because our new conservator couldn't be there that day. I had all my gear set up to photograph a little stone figure that belongs to the Maori Queen . . ."

"What do you mean, it belongs to the Queen? Doesn't it belong to the museum?"

"It's complicated. The museums do own the objects but they

only own them in trust for the Maori people. You know, since they *are* their ancestors and all, nobody else can own your great-uncle Harry, right? So the museums are sort of keeping them 'in trust for.' You can see I'm not real clear on it either, but in most cases this dual ownership arrangement seems to be a general thing. In Waikato though, there is this one figure that is specifically owned by the Queen."

"Okay. I guess that makes sense."

"So I'm just about to click the shutter and the lights go out in the whole museum."

"You're joking?"

"I'm not. It was—I swear—a half second before I snapped the picture."

"Well, what happened, for God's sake?"

"The museum director or assistant director or whoever he was—and this guy is not even a Maori—looks at me real serious and says, 'I'm going to check the fuse box, but I suggest that if it happens again you don't attempt to photograph this object.' Well, I'd been warned before I got there that this figure was especially tapu, which means sacred, and I'd been through so much strange stuff by then I said I wouldn't even draw it! I said I'd just do a written condition report."

"Did the lights come back on?"

"Yes, and I was a little nervous, but I tried again and took eight shots of him. Nothing else happened. It was just one hell of a weird coincidence."

Lesley the next day:

"What were you saying before the phone rang?"

"That there's a problem with the loan of this one piece—look, tell me if I'm boring you with all this."

"Don't be silly. I'm riveted!"

"Okay, tell me if you change your mind. So there's this one piece called Uenuku and I've been told it's the most important symbol of Maori power and spirituality that exists. It's also the most valuable piece in the show. They want it insured for five million dollars."

"Five million dollars!"

"Christ, don't tell everyone! In fact, be sure you don't spread that around."

"Sorry. What the hell is this thing made of, solid gold?"

"It's made of wood. It's not a matter of what it's made of, it's a matter of its importance. The story as I understand it is that Uenuku was a god who came in the form of a rainbow with the first canoes that brought the Maori people to the islands of New Zealand. When they got here the carving we now know was made and Uenuku was asked to dwell in it so that the elders could talk to him. It hasn't left New Zealand since."

"And you're taking this thing out of here?"

"Well, that's the problem. In this case it's the museum that doesn't want it to go. They say it's too valuable and too fragile and too important. I happen to think they're right."

"Yes, it's easy to see their point. Do the Maoris want it to go?"

"Yes, in fact the Maori Queen stepped in and said if the exhibition is to go at all it must be led by the spirit of Uenuku. You see, as he once led the Maori people to New Zealand . . ."

"This is amazing! Where is this thing?"

"It's in Te Awamutu. It is a wonderful story, isn't it? There is such a battle raging now between the museum administration and the Maori people that we had to go there incognito. Peta had said we shouldn't go at all, but it seemed worth it to at least get a close look even if we couldn't inspect and measure and photograph it."

"It is truly a wonderful story. Did you get to see it?"

"Yes, it's incredibly elegant, about eight feet high and very stark and simple."

Lesley the day after that:

"Any stories today?"

"Yes, there's more about this piece Uenuku, but you're going to think I'm crazy."

"No I won't, go ahead and spit it out."

"Well, even if you don't, I already think I'm crazy, so feel free to join me. The museum is very tiny and Uenuku is definitely the dominant object in the room. We walked in as tourists and started to look around. This thing just pulled me across the room. I stood in front of it by myself for a long time and just couldn't seem to break away. I found myself talking to it . . ."

"They're going to take you off in a net if you don't get away from these Maoris soon."

"I told you you'd think I was nuts. I was not talking out loud, though. Only in my head."

"Thank God for that!"

"Anyway, I just stood there and found myself asking it if this is okay. You know, I've come to some different thinking about the whole idea of this exhibition. I'm no longer sure it's a good idea."

"Did you get an answer from it?"

"Not really. But I'll tell you this, there is no doubt in my mind at all that there was something else—no, not something, *some-one* else, in that room."

December 9, 1982, Auckland, N.Z.

Jamie Summers
New York, U.S.A.

Dear Jamie,

You were right. This country and these people certainly make *us* look like the primitives when it comes to spirituality, intuition—I don't even know how to identify it. I myself have had some far more specific episodes of tapping into all this than I've yet had. (You can say "I told you so" when I get home.) I find it all emotionally exhausting and as I said, I'm just really sad. I wish I knew why. Can you tell I'm a bit confused these days?

See you real soon. I can't wait to be home.

Love,

Carol

*   *   *   *   *

It is the last day. I shower and put on my clothes. Then I stand in front of the mirror for a long time and stare at myself thinking that it is the last day and I have just showered and put on my clothes. I knock on my colleague's door and go to breakfast. It is raining.

For breakfast there is tea, thick as stew, black as ink. "Bring hot water," I say again, "I cannot drink this," and pour one quarter tea to three quarters water, and drink this with toast and jam. I watch people ladle canned spaghetti onto their toast and think that I will have this strange adventure indefinitely.

When we arrive at the museum we are escorted into a formal room with dark panelling and, there, are introduced to serious people in dark suits. They are the board of trustees and a few others and they are much older than I. We all sit around a tremendously long table of very dark wood and the dark suits begin to ask me questions. I am calm and answer the questions well. I answer all the questions I can and when there is one that I cannot answer I say, "I cannot answer that." This goes on for a very long time because the dark suits want to make absolutely certain they have satisfied themselves. Eventually they have.

Everyone stands up. I shake their hands and smile and there is nothing in my mind when I am not speaking. When I am not speaking I cast around in my mind for some thoughts and am amused that I can find none.

The director of the museum suggests tea and I say fine when I want to say no. Some of the dark suits leave but the rest of us go next door. There, under the fluorescent lights, we discuss small, inconsequential things. There is nothing more of importance to be said to these people.

Soon I stand up and nod to the dark young man who looks more Italian than I do and to the other dark young man who is the conservator. "We still have a lot to discuss," I say. "We should go back." Goodbyes are said and I leave the massive stone building with some heaviness in my body. I do not look back at the building but for a moment I pause, in the rain, and look out at the angry grey sea. There is still nothing in my mind, but the heaviness increases. I cannot explain this feeling and I do not try.

In a café near the hotel we sit for half an hour and talk. We talk about important things and when these things are done we talk about small, inconsequential things. I feel myself beginning to lose control. I look at the one man of whom I have become fond and at the other, who has been my defender and my spokesman. I look at them carefully. "Soon," I think, "I will be twelve thousand miles away. Soon I will have to question myself daily to be sure that they even exist." I stand up abruptly now. "I have to pack," I say in a voice that is too loud and a little shrill. I shake hands and say goodbye. "Here is my card," I say. "Look me up if you are ever in New York."

I am talking too fast. I know that if I am to look at their faces for the last time then this must be the last. Not almost the last. Not always the moment just before the last. Not missing all the words in anticipation of the terrible jolt of the last. They stand too and say goodbye and I think they look bewildered but I turn away now. I push the elevator button and then run down the stairs while they try to offer a ride. I know that I cannot wait for the elevator. I run and walk and run back to my room through the drizzle and when I get in the door I am out of breath. For a moment I thank God that my colleague and I have finally gotten separate rooms.

Then I begin to cry. At first I sit stiffly on the edge of the bed. My knees are straight out in front. My hands grip the edge of the mattress and I cry this way, softly, for some minutes. Slowly the sobs become louder and I lean farther and farther forward. The sobs go deeper yet and soon I am folded in half, hugging my knees. My body is wrenching now, tortured with sobs.

I cry deeply. I cry for myself, for dark young men, and for New Zealand women whom I met in New York. I cry for six weeks of not crying and I cry for beauty and for a beautiful brown man in Christchurch. I cry for all these things and then I cry for endings. I also cry for beginnings. I cry until the rain that has been pelting down all day lets up. The sky begins to clear and my tears take the place of the drops over Rangitoto Island and the harbor.

I am aware that hours are passing and do not care, but eventually I stand up. My body is no longer racked now and I carefully take off my clothes and fold them into the suitcase. I take out the other clothes that I will wear in the morning and place them, with great care, on the chair. I zip the bag and set it by the door and then I go into the bathroom and wash my face. I stare at my face for a long time in the mirror and I am not surprised not to recognize the face. Soon I stop trying to. I feel alternately and sometimes at once, important and strong and powerful, unloved, abandoned and always, always, emotionally isolated. I climb into the bed and curl tightly in on myself. There, in that way, I fall quietly asleep.

In the morning I sit on the plane waiting. I wait calmly but there is a desperate feeling in my chest. Soon the plane begins to taxi and it cannot move fast enough for me. I will the wheels to lift. I focus all the energy I have on willing the wheels to lift off the ground, to take me away from this land and back to a place where I know something. Where I know anything.

Eventually the nose of the plane tips up and I sense that the wheels have lifted. I release a breath so long and so deep that my chest and then my stomach slowly cave in. Only then do I realize that I have not been breathing.

THREE

The Seed

Fourteen months went by. They were punctuated as follows.

In Sydney, sitting under gauzy mosquito netting, I watched a screaming white cockatoo on the windowsill and made lists. All the people I'd met in the last months; the things I'd seen; all the hard things and all the easy things and all the things I'd done at all; stacked one on top of the other and filled pages of my journal. On the beaches the lists piled high. All the places I'd ever been and all the places I'd been while working for AFA; the ones I liked; the ones I hated; my friends; the cities and countries they lived in and all the exciting things I'd ever done.

Lists piled so high that a city of stacks grew in my mind. Sometimes the city exploded, spraying names and places into the blackness. There they hung, like dots of light. They mingled together and at those times were not part of neat and separate lists, but one long list—the things of which I was made. I felt wonderful. This surprised me.

I could have stayed in Sydney. There seemed no reason to leave. There was Margot, equal in every way to the memories I had held of her for seven years, her lovely flat overlooking the harbor and grocery shopping in the outdoor market on Saturdays. There were colleagues and at last, there was a place to stop and unpack my bags. Something had been whispering for a long time, something about moving on, making changes. By the time I left Sydney I felt so changed by the last few months that going home looked like going backwards. It depressed me.

On December 20, I landed at JFK Airport and took a cab right to the American Federation of Arts Christmas party. There were almost 300 people there. Wearing a suntan, a flannel shirt and corduroy pants, and carrying all my luggage, I burst in the door. I was scooped up in joy by my friends and colleagues and wondered how I could ever think of leaving. After that emotional shift there was no more predicting my moods. Once I had been joyously even. Now, some days found me crazy about New York, my job, my life; others wanting to flee.

My friend Jamie spoke quietly, but like a bulldozer, too. She said I was confused because my own intuition was beginning to surface. We'd been going on about this for nearly two years. It was nothing really specific, just strange shifts in perception. There were moments when I saw through things—something like that. The room would disappear, the things people were saying became transparent. I could see, or maybe feel, something else that was going on underneath and when this happened I felt very isolated. I was, for a moment, on the outside peering back in. The separateness frightened me sometimes. It made me angry sometimes.

Jamie and I talked about it all the time. "Focused intuition," she said. "You can learn to use this. When are you going to accept your own ability?" A fierce battle raged in quiet, contemplative tones in Indian restaurants; at her loft while she made lemon pies for her teenage son, Garry; at my apartment. About the intuition, I said, "Baloney!" I found clear, rational explanations for everything. It was fine for her, she was an artist. She was a Californian hippie who kept bees in her loft on Broome Street!

Sure, she could get up every morning and meditate. Me? I wanted to get up every morning and run. I wanted to feel the ground being pounded under my feet, feel the wind and get rained and snowed on. I wanted to live on the earth, which is something Jamie didn't seem to do very much of the time. "Focused intuition," she called it. She did "readings" on people and also helped them develop their own intuition. I felt I was fighting to hold on to something that was familiar, to a way I knew how to be. A door had been pried open and I fought to pull it shut.

"She's nice," other friends said, "but I'm surprised you'd have a friend like that. She's so spacy, and you're so specific, or something." It surprised me, too.

Christmas came and went. 1983 arrived. Life seemed to be all about Maoris and I worked like a fiend. We all did at the office because we'd never dreamed an exhibition could be so complicated. Our application for government indemnity had to be in Washington by April 1st. It was still more than a year before I would go back to New Zealand and pack the exhibition, but every single detail had to be planned, reviewed, refined and scrutinized before we wrote it into the application. This plan and the cultural significance of the project would be the deciding factors. Once indemnity is awarded, the details of the approved plan can be changed only with formal review by the indemnity panel.

I had the opportunity to feel strong again, to show everybody what I was good at, which was organizing and making sound, rational judgments. I juggled hundreds of details that didn't seem to fit anywhere and found places where they fit. This show was just sufficiently bigger, more valuable and complicated than all the others I'd done, and the consequences of my actions enough more serious as to make it all newly exhilarating. I devised elaborate schemes, wrote exhaustive exploratory letters, telexed New Zealand and Australia, putting critical deadlines on requests for information. It was exciting stuff.

The rolls of film we'd shot in New Zealand went out for processing—just contact sheets to see how everything had turned out. It would be months and months before I needed prints. Even with such bad conditions in most of the museums the photographs were very good. All eight shots of the Queen's stone figure were perfect. "Look at this!" I said, suddenly remembering when I saw them. I told my assistant and one of the secretaries how the lights had gone out in Waikato and they laughed and made "spook" jokes.

I laughed too, but that was when I first started to notice something strange. Looking at those pictures made me sad, or nostalgic, or something I didn't really understand. There suddenly seemed a tremendous distance between an office on 65th Street and a small museum in Waikato. I was sad about that distance. I hardly recognized the person standing in the darkened museum. I could hear her seriously discussing the issue with the museum person. I could see her, when he left the room, standing silently in the dark near the small figure called a life-force container, acknowledging it as she might a stranger whose language she did not speak. Now I could see her, in an office in the city, giggling over something that fell outside her usual way of understanding. It made me want to cry while everyone around me laughed. The phone started ringing then as it did nearly every five minutes. I answered it and a few seconds later my mind was completely back in Manhattan. If asked, I would have denied having seen beyond—having possibly had some small insight into another way of being.

Peta was coming to New York at the end of April for meetings at AFA and the Metropolitan Museum; then to St Louis and San Francisco for more meetings. Jane Tai and I would go with him for those. Jane, the Associate Director of AFA, was one of my good friends. We planned ten days of vacation in California once Peta went back to New Zealand.

Jamie said she'd founded something called the Center for Investigative Studies of Intuition. It sounded like a nice enough idea. I didn't know what was legally required to found something but suspected that Jamie had said, "I hereby found," and then had stationery printed at the While-You-Wait offset place on the corner of Broadway. Members of the Center met monthly at her loft.

I'd been seeing Jamie often. She was making some headway with me whether I wanted to admit it or not. We had long, involved conversations about intuition and human energy, about metamorphosis and about information. A little at a time I started to see that what she was talking about, her "work" as she called it, was not hocus pocus at all but a very real and useful way of life. Now she invited me to attend this more public forum. "It sounds great," I said and was always too busy on the nights they met.

At the office I continued to work frantically on the preparation of the indemnity application, starting by designing packing crates. Of the 174 objects, some were so big they would be packed by themselves. That was the easy part. Having measured them in New Zealand I now needed only to allow the right amount of space around them to come up with the inner dimensions of the crate. The rest of the objects were smaller and would be packed in groups, taking four things into account: size, weight, value and lender. It was like working a jigsaw puzzle to see that things fit well together, were not off balance; that no one crate carried extraordinary value while another carried little and that one crate did not contain objects all owned by the same museum. That way, if something happened to one crate, each museum stood to lose only a few pieces rather than one losing all.

We were working on twelve other exhibitions at the same time. I was becoming exhausted in spite of the adrenalin that kept me going. Life seemed to consist entirely of AFA exhibitions relieved only by long runs in the park and intense conversations with friends.

Jamie the artist was inspired by the concept of metamorphosis. Her drawings and avant garde sculpture always explored transformation—something in the process of becoming something else. The bees she kept were part of this fascination—their daily voyages out the window in search of pollen, their nightly return carrying a substance that would evolve into honey; the idea of cross-pollination—one tiny being touching down, randomly linking things together by virtue of what it takes away or leaves behind.

Her conceptual research was not without dangers, of course. Once I asked Garry why his arm was swollen. "My mother," he said, looking at her sternly, "managed to drop the hive." Her laughter pealed out and she became a mischievous child. "It's *not* funny, mother," he said. But you could tell by the corners of his mouth that he thought it was funny too.

Hearing that Peta was coming to New York, Jamie asked if I would invite him to speak at one of her monthly intuition meetings. She was convinced that an artist's energy is transferred into the work of art in the process of creation, the process being a metamorphosis in itself. She'd read a lot about the Maori people and knew that they live this idea daily. I was proud and flattered but embarrassed to ask Peta. I'd never had any conversations with him about intuition. As far as I could tell, the Maori people didn't think about intuition at all. They thought they were normal. Mostly, I was embarrassed and afraid to have anyone at my office find out. They would think I was crazy, or worse, unprofessional.

My courage was non-existent. I told Jamie I'd have to think about it for a while. I threw myself back into my work and proceeded not to think about it at all.

Eventually, a final plan for the collection, packing, transport and care of the Maori exhibition emerged from the mass of details. An art packer named Brian Wood, a man I'd finally located during my first visit to Auckland, would build all the outer crates in New Zealand using my dimensions and drawings. He would deliver the empty crates to the two packing sites—the Auckland Museum and the Auckland City Art Gallery. In April, May and June of 1984 I would spend eight weeks in Auckland with our New York art packer, Sam Martelli, carefully fitting each object into its packing crate. Brian Wood, the New Zealand packer and Gavin Johnson, the conservator from our first trip, would become assistant packers. In mid-June three planes would finally roll down the runway in Auckland. When their wheels lifted off they would take 174 treasured Maori artifacts, for the first time, off their native soil. From that moment on, my life would not be my own. The application was complete. We mailed it to Washington.

Peta arrived on April 30, my thirtieth birthday. He'd never been to New York before and I planned to show him what there was to love about my city. I introduced him to good friends and together we took him to the Rainbow Room for a drink, to see *Porgy and Bess* at Radio City Music Hall (this he loved because he had once sung in a New Zealand production of it), to see the Alvin Ailey dance company at City Center (this he was enthralled by because his wife was a former choreographer) and to Arthur Miller's *A View from the Bridge* on Broadway (over which he cried). I took him to visit my family in New Jersey. There, we inadvertently discovered that his great-grandfather and my mother's family came from the same town in Italy.

During meetings at the office, Peta told us that the battle still raged over the loan of Uenuku. It was an ancestor of such tremendous mana, such spiritual presence and power, that the debate would be taken to prime ministerial level if necessary. The time to finalize our list of loans was drawing very close but we all agreed that for an object so critical to the exhibition it was worth waiting out the battle until the very last minute. He confirmed that a large group of Maoris, including an official group of about twenty elders, would have to be brought to the States to perform dawn ceremonies at each of the three museums on the tour. The highest officials of the AFA and the hosting museums would be expected there and later, breakfast would have to be served to all, sealing the ceremony according to Maori custom.

We tiptoed around the issue of who would cover these enormous, unbudgeted expenses. Everyone tried hard to accept, but it seemed could never really comprehend, the spiritual needs of the Maori people. This was understandable. Peta, I think never really grasped the depth of the American's inability to understand. He said things almost casually, with no apology and little explanation as if, of course, we had some counterpart in our culture, as if it were only the fine details that had to be worked out. I floated between the two ways of thinking, unable to find the place where I belonged, wanting to help and not having the words. Neither did I have the courage.

Later in the week, meetings moved to the Met. There, among other things, we discussed the possible routes the procession of elders would take on their way from Fifth Avenue to the Sackler balcony in which the exhibition would be installed, where the ceremony and opening reception would take place and where the breakfast would be served. The courtyard of the Temple of Dendur was suggested for some of the events. It is a huge space and from there it would be possible to just see the Maori exhibition in the balcony above. Peta listened. He listened for a long time as everyone prowled around the courtyard discussing why it would or wouldn't be a good place. When he finally spoke, his voice was friendly and neutral, completely uninflected. "This is an Egyptian marae," he said. "Their mana is very strong here."

So neutral was the statement that it was impossible to read his thoughts, to know if this was a good thing or bad. We looked from him back to the temple and tried to read him, to see what it was he wanted from us. His words drew my eyes to the temple, across the stone floors that surrounded it, up the sweeping glass wall that separated it from the trees of Central Park, through the planes of light that slanted across it. In front of me now, strong Egyptian hands set stones, one on top of the other, building a temple that would stand for centuries on the Nile. Generations of hands caressed and lingered over the stones as they passed through the door. I stared. Resonant voices crept from dark spaces deep inside the temple, their murmuring surrounding me in a cocoon of sound. I could hear nothing else. Entire lifetimes seemed to flow around the temple like a powerful river, like the Nile.

It seemed impossible. How many times before had I stood in

front of this temple? But I had looked without seeing, or perhaps had looked with the intention of seeing what I expected to. Peta looked with the intention of seeing what was there.

Someone moved then, or coughed or spoke. Barely a moment had gone by. Peta said something else ånd we began moving slowly away, discussing the possibility of using the museum cafeteria and the great entrance hall for some of the events.

At the door I turned and looked back at the temple. I stared at it, tried to pierce its walls. I looked for hands and listened for voices, but it was just a stone temple. Soft planes of light slanted across its face. I turned, and before even crossing the threshold, had begun to deny the whole experience.

There were about twenty people at Jamie's loft on the night Peta was to speak. I did not know the people and hardly anyone spoke in the few minutes before Jamie said we were going to begin. There were no social exchanges, few words, little laughter, but still the room drew us in, welcoming. Everything waited. The chairs and the walls, the drawings on the walls and the people—some in jeans, others in business clothes, having come right from work—sat quietly and waited. Peta, wearing a red sweatshirt that said "Maori Festival" in small letters on the front, sat on the willow-branch sofa made by gypsies in California, with Jamie next to him on the wooden chair with a copper seat in which she always preferred to sit. The rest of us sat on the floor.

Jamie asked me to explain about the exhibition and how Peta came to be there. When I finished, everyone turned to him. Peta opened his mouth to speak and began to cry instead. Quickly he stood and walked to the end of the loft. Eyes followed him in surprise and then turned away, leaving him to blow his nose and dry his eyes. He was smiling and sniffling when he returned. "Forgive me," he said. "I'll be all right. It was just like going home for a minute." We knew that he had felt the energy in the room.

Peta sat down again and told the ancient Maori myth of

creation in which Sky Father, Rangi-nui and Earth Mother, Papatuanuku gave birth to the gods. During the eons that Rangi and Papa lay together the universe was dark and still and very cold. Rangi clothed his woman with trees and plants to warm her, and as the temperature on earth rose, the life of the creatures began and Papa gave birth to their sons, the gods. The god-children lived in darkness, trapped between their parents for some time until Tane, the god of the forests, convinced his brothers that they must force their parents apart. This they did, and although it allowed light to flood into the world, it is said that Rangi still laments the divorce with his tears, the rain. In the new atmosphere of light and warmth, Tane went on to create the first woman while his brothers made fish, the winds, evil and disease, war and peace. Tane slept with the woman, making her pregnant, and the generations of man began. Peta explained how in all the generations that followed, people have had to divide their awareness between Rangi and Papa. From Sky Father come clarity, peace of mind and inspiration; but it is not possible to live "up there" all the time. It is necessary to live equally comfortably in the company of Earth Mother, Papa. We must feed our children and pay our mortgages. We must take the bus to work. This, Peta said, explains why all sacred Maori ceremonies are sealed by the sharing of food, bringing people back to earth after a visit with Rangi.

Peta spoke as if to himself. We listened with equal distance, each silently enveloped in an unreachable place of our own. He explained that it had been difficult for the Maori people to discuss their art with the Americans. There is no single word for art in the Maori language. A piece of wood has no significance. It is transformed through the art process. The contact with people, the words and stories built into the piece of wood during its making and in the centuries that might follow, turn it into a taonga, something treasured. The object is actually clothed with words, animated and transformed into a cultural object whose mana, or psychic force and power, are increased by continued association with people and events during its lifetime.

Peta talked and talked into the stillness. He talked about the natural forces in each of us, forces that guide us and show us which way to go if we know how to listen. He talked about finding the center of those natural forces, of finding our balance. Sometimes he cried and we cried. Everyone was suspended in the silence of the room. His truth was overwhelming. His spirit was overwhelming and some information greater than the words he had spoken was passed to us that evening. Slowly we made a reluctant passage back to find nearly two hours gone by. Jamie had prepared food and gently, as we ate, we began to talk and laugh. We asked him questions. Soon we were all once again within the strong embrace of Papa, having almost forgotten our splendid conversation with Rangi. But this was as it should be.

Meetings at the St. Louis Art Museum and the deYoung Museum in San Francisco were proud and gracious and professional. Surprisingly, the people there didn't seem quite as many light years away from understanding what Peta and the Maori people were all about. It made me begin to wonder about New York. At an elegant dinner in St. Louis there were speeches by the museum's director, a trustee, and by Peta, who spoke in Maori and then in English. When he had finished, the mood began to shift away from formality and speech-making. I found myself standing. "I'd like to say something," I said, wondering what that could be. Sixteen pairs of eyes were suddenly fixed on me. I opened my mouth, hoping something intelligent was going to come out. "When I was in New Zealand," I said, smiling directly at Peta, "I was not allowed to speak publicly for six weeks. Once, in Hawkes Bay, Peta made very special arrangements and I was allowed to say 'Hello,' and even 'Thank you.' " I was grinning by then. "I don't have very much to say now, but had to get up and say *something*." Everyone else was grinning too, but also cautiously watching Peta to see if he would be offended. He looked at me in wonder for a moment and then began to giggle. The room relaxed. "I just wanted to say," I went on, turning away from Peta and looking at the others, "that what you have involved yourselves in is not an exhibition. It is an experience that will change you. Something very special is about to happen." I sat down feeling privileged and very proud.

By the time Peta left for New Zealand everyone was in love with him and with the Maori people. Jane and I saw him off in San Francisco and then spent ten days driving around California and the Mojave desert. On May 14th I wrote in my journal: "Pasos Robles, California. I've finally 'gone public.' Explained a bit to Jane today about Jamie and my intuition work. I amazed myself by being reasonably articulate and not sounding like a fool. Most significant is that telling her made it real for me—stopped feeling silly about it. It's just something I do. Maybe there's room for it to exist now."

When we got back to New York, life was all about ancient pottery from the Mimbres Valley in New Mexico and Renaissance gilded silver. I began carefully orchestrating the complicated assembly of the pottery from points all around the country and the packing and transport of the silver, a collection that would take me for a second time to London.

The Maori exhibition was dormant. We waited for word from the Indemnity Board.

Jamie asked about the possibility of organizing a public symposium with the elders when they came for the opening in September of 1984. More people, she said, should have a chance to experience what a handful of us had with Peta the night at her loft. But I was on my guard again. "It's a fine idea," I said. I told her she could write to Peta directly about it, I would give her the address. Of course, it couldn't involve AFA at all. We were all far too busy and there was no possibility of adding another event to our planning.

I said there was a good chance, too, that no one there would have much interest in such an event. These things were true, yet still, I was saddened by the depth of my own cowardice.

That Thursday Jamie was riding her bike in Greenwich Village. She lost her balance and fell under the wheels of a garbage truck. She died instantly. She was 35.

The night after she died I had a powerful and disturbing dream. I had become pregnant and casually ignored the fact until suddenly, in the seventh month, I realized with horror that I would soon have the child. I didn't want the child. There was a tremendous sense of being swept along, of too-lateness, of being unable to alter a path chosen in an earlier time frame. There was terror. I continued to run hard every day despite my mother's warnings. I hoped against hope that I would miscarry. There was no ending to the dream, but I awoke knowing that I had had the child.

The dream was transparent to me. The child, my intuition, had been growing in me, ignored for some time, but was finally acknowledged in horror and fear for what it might mean to my life. Attempts to push it away had failed and as the arrival of the child was sensed but never clearly defined in the dream; so the intuition was there. I remembered no delivery.

*   *   *   *   *

Friends don't know what to do with you when your grief is larger than they think it should be. I paid a price for my cowardice. They would never know what Jamie had been to me.

While sorting and packing her belongings at the loft we found her appointment book. It was a six-month calendar, ending on June 30, 7:30 P.M., the day and the time she died. There were no pages beyond that.

The willow-branch sofa was placed on the pile of things to be discarded. It was too big for anyone, in their grief and confusion, to know how to cope with. I found someone with a van and took it home.

I remembered a beekeeper, a sweet, Chinese man in my hometown in New Jersey. I had not spoken to him in ten years, but I called and he came that night to take the hive. A week later the beekeeper called me back. The queen bee had gotten away, he said. The entire colony followed, disappearing into the woods in the town where I grew up. He had, he said, never lost a queen bee before.

Jamie did not talk about her past. Now it turned out that her body was to be shipped to her home town of Pasos Robles, California for burial. I had never heard of Pasos Robles until the day Jane and I wandered through and decided to stay at the inn. There, in a coffee shop across from the small cemetery, I had first told Jane about my work with Jamie.

Word came from Washington. US Government Indemnity had been awarded for the Maori exhibition. I threw myself into the work that this announcement created. Now that our plan was approved it had to be set in motion. But I could not work hard enough to deaden my grief. I cried at the smallest things, in the most unlikely places, crying, I think, mostly for me.

The willow sofa looked huge and out of place in my apartment. I threw out an old armchair to make it fit but still, it did not. Jamie's presence hung thickly from its branches. I slept with the light on, could not sleep at all. She might come here, broken and bloodied. She might sit on this sofa and talk to me! I draped one of my scarves over it, threw newspapers on its seat. I tried to make it look as if it belonged. Nothing worked. I could not go near it.

Death became a fascination. I was afraid I would die, my father would die, my sister. I was afraid of traffic, of airplanes. I was also morbidly energized by this death, watching it, as a child might a bruised knee. When a scab began to form I picked, probed with delicious fear, knowing it would bleed again.

I waited for a scar.

The idea of returning to New Zealand became an obsession. I planned with meticulous detail my approaching trip to London to pack and courier the Renaissance silver. With less care and no enthusiasm I threw together a rough plan for the three-week vacation I was to spend in Europe before arriving in London. The thought had once filled me with excitement, but now I watched blandly as the date approached, wanting only to return to New Zealand. I did not fully understand this.

The need for change, dormant since my return from Sydney, once again began to surface. I boldly announced to my friends that I was moving and began the search for a new apartment, disgusted with myself for having lived so long in such a tiny place. It was time to make changes in a major way.

My job too, lost some of the temporary gloss I had polished back over it in the last months. Once it had been my life. Now I shifted in and out of fierce and opposing feelings.

On July 15th I wrote this letter to my friend Doris through whom I had met Jamie years before.

For Doris . . .

You are lucky never to have seen the place where she lived. It cannot haunt you now as it does me.

My mind goes there several times a day and climbs the steep steps. They are grey. (They were always grey, even before she died, so you need not attach any importance.)

The stairs start from right inside the street door and go up so far and so steep I don't think I've ever craned my neck up there to see where they end. They pause for a breather half way up, at a landing of sorts, and that's where Jamie's door is. Metal, and very wide.

The door is not locked and I enter boldly because I have so much fear. The emptiness leaps at me, shouts and waves its arms hoping to scare me away, but I will not go. I cower near the threshold and after a short time am able to start moving around.

I note that the windows are closed now. That looks wrong, as I have never seen them closed before. It would be nice if there were some bits of abandoned clutter but someone has cleaned very thoroughly. Things look white and the loft seems bigger than it used to. Small sounds take on great importance and alarmingly, there is no punctuation in the light. It washes in from the north in broad slabs and reproduces itself exactly on the floor boards. Uninterrupted. I stare at my watch a lot here, for long moments, not without some panic, and only when I am satisfied that the long hand has made progress do I release a breath.

The room was never very crowded with furnishings, even then, and with a quick turn of the mind I can recreate it. The problem is holding on. The willow couch with its back to the windows gets a little watery and the drawings on the blank white wall start to swim almost immediately, no matter how hard I try to pin them in place with my eyes. It is usually when I notice that the bookcase I have imaged on the west wall still does not break the planes of light that the room goes empty. I become discouraged.

Sometimes Jamie stops by. She slips in quietly, almost tentatively. This is not her place any more and she doesn't want to intrude. She never proceeds much beyond the door, only stands there and darts her eyes into deep places we can't see. Her expression is unreadable. It makes me wish I knew her better. After a while she seems satisfied and slips quietly out. If I am in the front, I lean my head against one of the huge windows. I wait to see her come out the door onto Broome Street, and usually, I forget why I am waiting there.

It is not gentle, this place where she lived. I am glad you never had the opportunity to know it. It gives me no peace from myself.

Postscript. The bees have all gone. Only their soft hum remains. It lingers, suspended as a backdrop of quietude for all that is about to happen.

With those few strokes of the pen, a chapter in my life somehow ended and another began.

*   *   *   *   *

On September 9 I left for my three-week holiday in Europe and to pack the silver exhibition in London. I explored Europe and I explored myself—slowly, over six weeks beginning to know a bit more about the person I'd become.

On Sunday, October 26, the job complete, I left London on a 747 freighter plane. We had on board four Clydesdales, six racehorses, 10,000 pounds of venison, four grooms for the horses and seven crates of Renaissance silver for which I was the courier. This turned into an extraordinary fifteen-hour adventure which so captured all I loved about my job and my life that once again, the thought of walking away from it was laughable. After this episode I surrendered in some small way to my state of confusion. It seemed appropriate, and no longer something to be judged.

During my absence the Maori exhibition was finally given an official name. The elders and officials had at last agreed on a title that was also satisfactory to AFA. Their first choice had been three lines long in Maori, followed by an English subtitle, and had meant something along the lines of "Art from the People of the Long White Cloud," Long White Cloud being the literal translation of Aotearoa, the Maori name for New Zealand.

With some humor we pointed out that exhibition titles in America tended to be a bit quicker and punchier. Also that it had to fit on the banner that would hang in front of the Met. The debate went on. Suggestions were made and rejected by one person or another for spiritual and political reasons that were beyond our comprehension, until finally the exhibition was named "Te Maori," meaning simply, The Maori. Its subtitle was "Maori Art from New Zealand Collections."

It was time to print the photos from my first trip to New Zealand. They would be used to prepare a condition notebook that was to travel with the exhibition throughout the tour. I carefully circled all the images we'd need on the contact sheets, matched them to their negatives and sent them off to the photographer.

The prints came back several weeks later—stacks of 5x7 black-and-whites. There was also a note from the photographer. "I don't know what happened," it said, "but several negatives were missing." I began to sort. Of some 400 photos, the only ones missing were the ones of the Queen's stone figure! I searched the files. I called the photographer. I decided those negatives had probably never been returned when I had the contact sheets printed almost a year before, but even as I searched, I knew it wasn't so. I'd had them in my hands and had in fact shown them to my assistant when telling her how the lights went out in Waikato.

"Who could have taken them!?" she said now. She was almost shouting, and looked bewildered. I was laughing. People gathered around in the office to see what the commotion was about. "Who could have taken just those," someone else said. "Look," I told them, "I don't think I can explain this, but no one took the negatives. He just didn't want to be photographed."

"That's crazy!" someone said. "You're crazy!" They laughed, but it was tentative, ambiguous laughter.

I found that I was delighted by this mischief. Each object was to have had a written condition report, and on the facing page of the notebook, a photograph. Across the blank photo page for that piece I scrawled, "REFUSED TO BE PHOTOGRAPHED!" Jamie would have approved!

After all the effort we'd put into getting US Government Indemnity, we now ran up against a brick wall. The Management Committee in Wellington, having reviewed a sample of the policy, politely informed us that it could not be accepted. As with all fine arts insurance policies, the indemnity coverage included in its provisions a "loss/buy-back" clause. In the event of total loss the value of the object is paid to the owner by the insurer. Once the money is paid, however, all rights of ownership automatically transfer to the insurer, giving them, in the

event of recovery, the right to sell the object at public auction.
The original owner can prevent this sale by paying the insurer
the market value of the object at the time of recovery. In either
case, the legal transfer of ownership gives the insurer a way to
recoup their money.

"Not possible!" said the Maori people. Rights of ownership
could never transfer to someone else. If this happened and the
object were ever recovered it would be dead and meaningless,
its mana having been destroyed by the change of hands. The
long-distance discussion that ensued turned into a battle, the
battle into a brick wall. No, it didn't matter that this was a
standard, unchangeable policy that had been accepted by every
other government to which it had ever been offered. Yes, the
Indemnity Board was sympathetic, but no, they would not be
able to waive or alter the clause. Yes, the New Zealand Government understood that they could not expect to have the money
and the object too. That was not what they were asking.

Weeks went by without resolution. Perhaps after seven years
of planning there would be no Maori exhibition. We continued
our work on the show, but with less enthusiasm than we once
had. As time passed, each of us adjusted in our own way to the
fact that the exhibition might be lost over a technical detail. I
became alternately morose, feeling New Zealand and all that it
represented slipping away, and inspired by the notion that
maybe it was time to leave. This seemingly terrible thing may
have happened to release me from my promise to the beautiful
brown man in Christchurch. Now, without the weight of responsibility, without the vision of his tears coursing down his brown
cheeks, I could leave AFA. I could leave New York and if I
wanted to I could go to New Zealand on my own.

At the worst times I relived the loss of Jamie all over again—
at night I sometimes curled up on the willow sofa, falling asleep
there as I prepared to accept this new loss.

Eventually the Indemnity Board made what was to be its final
offer in the rounds of proposals and counter-proposals about the
loss/buy-back clause. An alternative clause already existed in

the policy. It said that a recovered object, rather than being sold at auction, would be automatically returned to the original owner. The owner was then to pay the insurer the amount of money received at the time of loss. Only if the owner chose not to buy back the object could it be sold. This clause, it said, could be elected only by "a Sovereign or an agent of a Sovereign." In other words, the alternative could be chosen only if the objects were legally owned by a government or its agents.

Because of the complicated system of ownership and the fact that the artifacts were considered national treasures, it could be said that they were being lent under the auspices of the New Zealand Government. The Indemnity Board made an offer. For purposes of this exhibition, they said, the clause could be amended so that Sovereigns acting on behalf of agents could elect the clause as well as agents acting on behalf of Sovereigns. That way, the New Zealand Government, speaking for the museums, could choose the alternate clause. The difference was very subtle. We waited tensely for the response to our telexed offer. It would be the last try.

The Management Committee accepted. This surprised me. As far as I could see, the basis for the argument had not been changed at all. Both the clause and its alternate still clearly stated that all rights of ownership would transfer to the U.S. Government at the time of payment. The only difference was that one allowed for the automatic sale of the object unless it was prevented, the other for the automatic return unless it was refused. I said nothing, hoping there would never be reason to test my theory. Te Maori was back on track.

During the second week of February a telex arrived at the AFA. It read: "The loan of Uenuku has been secured, therefore he will participate in the exhibition." We rejoiced, but a knot began to form in my stomach. In the back of my mind I saw the tears glistening on brown cheeks, a strong hand reaching out to caress and give life to a bit of wood. Yes, I'll take care of them for you, I'd said that day, though no words were spoken. I had made promises I wasn't so sure I could keep.

On March 28 I had a final meeting with Sam, the art packer. "I keep having this nightmare, Sam," I said. "We're standing in Auckland and you're looking down at a tiny little crate and then up at a huge carving. You're saying, 'What did you have in mind with this one, Carol?' "

He laughed. "That's not going to happen," he said.

"It might happen, Sam! I measured those pieces once, in the dark, two years ago, and then I had a guy 12,000 miles away build a bunch of crates. It just might happen!"

On March 31 I ran six miles, showered, had breakfast, put the garbage out, changed the message on the phone machine, called a cab and left for Sydney, Australia.

FOUR

The Plant

A colleague in Sydney:

"Did you know there are three million people and sixty million sheep in New Zealand?"

"Yes, I'd heard that."

"Here we prefer to say that there are sixty-three million sheep in New Zealand and three million of them think they're people."

"That's what I like to hear—nice healthy rivalry. Shall I tell you the saying New Zealanders have about Australia? There they say, 'Australia, where men are men and sheep run scared.' "

"Oh, God."

Another colleague in Sydney:

"Eight weeks in New Zealand? Good God, whatever will you do there? One would be hard put to entertain oneself for a week in New Zealand."

"Well, I must admit, that's the way I felt about it last time I was there, but I've changed my tune. I'm really looking forward to it. Besides, considering what I'm supposed to accomplish in those eight weeks I won't have too much time to worry about entertaining myself."

A friend in Sydney:

"Where do you get virgin wool?"
   "I don't know, where?"
   "From ugly sheep."
   "Oh, God."

Margot:

"Did you find it difficult to be a woman working in New Zealand?"
   "I would call that an understatement."
   "I'm not surprised. I'd heard that New Zealand men are still quite behind the times in terms of chauvinism. I can't, in all honesty, say that Australian men are much better."
   "Well, I really found two different things going on in New Zealand. I sense a lot of chauvinism among white New Zealand males—the European New Zealanders. But the stuff with the Maori elders? That's pre-chauvinism. I don't even know what to call it, and for some reason it doesn't bother me as much."
   "Yes, I see your point. I can't define it either but it isn't as offensive."
   "To give you an example, I am less disturbed about the Maori custom of not allowing women to speak on the marae than I am by my white New Zealand friend's response to it. When I mentioned to him that this was the case, he wrinkled up his brow, looked at me, *truly* perplexed, and said, 'But why *should* they be allowed to speak?' "
   "Nice friend you've got there."
   "Margot, that is not atypical!"

A male friend in Sydney:

"Why did God make women?"
   "Why?"
   "Because sheep don't type."
   "OK, I've had enough with the sheep jokes now."

April 3, 1984, Sydney, Australia
The American Federation of Arts
New York, U.S.A.

Hi, guys . . .

Hope you're all enjoying those fluorescent office lights . . .

The trip took exactly 36 hours door-to-door and was pretty brutal. The highlight was an abalone dinner in L.A. with Ben Johnson. He picked me up at the airport to help fill the six hours between flights. The rest of the trip was a blur of canned air, bad airline food and a constant, dull pressure in the head.

I forgot the pain of it very quickly though. It is glorious here. I arrived late yesterday afternoon, was up at six o'clock this morning for a run in the Domain (their version of Central Park), and was on the beach by 10:30. They say fall set in last week but for my arrival it seems to have reverted back to summer.

Margot and I are having a lovely time lolling around in her spacious, sunny flat overlooking the harbor. Giant white cockatoos sometimes come and screech on the windowsill at dawn and I have to keep pinching myself to be sure I'm really here. We're having dinner with a friend of mine—a conservator from the Art Gallery of New South Wales—to dinner with friends of Margot's on Thursday and away for a four-day weekend in the country on Friday. We're heading north to Byron Bay.

By now you all hate me. Don't plot your revenge yet, though. I may well pay for my sins when I hit New Zealand.

Love and kisses to all,
Carol

April 9, 1984, Sydney, Australia
The American Federation of Arts
New York, U.S.A.

Dear everyone,

We just returned from our four-day weekend. It turned out to be an adventure that gave even me a run for my money. Margot does not drive so I drove 1250 miles this weekend. We picked a fine time to go off. The first day was beautiful, hot and sunny. Then there was the monsoon. It monsooned for three days.

We had a fabulous weekend! We passed kangaroos on the road! It was like being on Mars, especially since the terrain itself is not unlike Pennsylvania or New York State. Rolling hills, green valleys, and where we would have "Deer Crossing" signs, they have "Kangaroo Crossing" signs! There were some bodies of dead roos that had been hit by cars and one night, a cute little one just sitting by the side of the road.

I feel as if I've been away six weeks already. Tomorrow night we've been invited to the opening of the Sydney Biennial at the Art Gallery.

What astonishes and delights me is how Margot and I can be such good and easy friends considering the minuscule amount of time we have actually spent together over the last nine years. There was the year she spent in New York, where we met in '75, seven years of occasional letters, the two weeks I spent in Sydney in '82 after New Zealand, and now this visit. Extraordinary to think that we are as comfortable with each other as with friends we each see every day. Sometimes we talk, sometimes we're just quiet, sometimes we argue and often we giggle like fools. Delightful!

By the time you get this I'll be in New Zealand. Lots more letters from there . . .

Love,
Carol

Margot:

"Were you actually aware of rivalry between New Zealand and Australia?"

"Absolutely! Most of it is pretty good-natured, but some is serious stuff. My first proposal to the Te Maori Management Committee involved bringing an Australian art packer to Auck-

land to be the assistant to our packer from New York. It was
flatly turned down."

"That's amazing!"

"Yes, I was pretty amazed. Especially since I'm sure I mentioned before I left New Zealand last time that I was stopping in
Australia to research possible packing facilities. Nobody told
me not to bother. You remember all those meetings I had here
last time? Well, I shouldn't have bothered."

"But you say you *are* bringing your New York packer down."

"That seems to be different. Bringing in a New Yorker is
acceptable. Bringing in an Australian is not."

      *   *   *   *   *

It is time for my friend to leave. We stand at the door and can
think of nothing to say. We can think of nothing that means
anything that would be worth saying. I look at my friend whom
I love. I look at this friend who will walk out the door and go to
work now as she does every morning. I will not see her this
evening when she comes home from work because soon after
she goes I will pick up my bags and walk out the door to go to
the airport. From there I will go to New Zealand and from there
eventually to New York, and if I ever see this friend again, it will
be a very, very long time from now.

I am choking a little now and being too casual and she is
blinking a little too often now and being too casual. "Have a
good day," I say. "If I leave anything behind you can mail it
to me."

"Have a safe trip," she says. "Write to me when you get
there. I can't wait to hear how it goes."

And then she leaves. We have a last hug without really
looking at each other and she walks out the door.

I begin to cry and wonder why I did not cry while she was
still here. I feel the wrenching, the gut-ripping feeling that I
know well. It is the same feeling that I had two weeks ago at my

going-away party in New York. I wonder how many more times
I can do this. I know that if I leave this job it will not be because
I am tired. It will not be because I am bored. If I leave, it will be
because I cannot stand the wrenching too many more times. I
begin to walk around the flat.

I linger at the window, staring at the harbor below. There
are green ships and white sails and I burn the window, the
harbor, the ships and the white sails into my brain. I pause for a
moment in the bedroom. I pause long enough to see the huge
wicker laundry hamper and the chaos of my friend's closet with
her brightly colored clothes. I sear these things, and the way
the light washes across the room, into my brain and then I
move into the kitchen. I open the door to the fire escape and
stand there, next to yesterday's garbage. I can see the Art
Gallery off in the distance where it sits among trees in the
Domain. On the lawn there are specks of white that I know to be
cockatoos. I take a deep breath and when I go back inside I have
an idea.

Quickly I begin to cut small squares of paper from a lined
pad. As the idea grows I work faster, frantically. I cut and cut
until I have maybe 30 squares and on each I write the date.
"April 16, 1984," I write, and then a small note, a thought on
each of the squares. "Thinking of you today," one says. "Hi,
how are you this morning?" another. I write and write until
each of the squares has a different note and is signed with love
and then I begin to hide the notes. In the page of her book where
the marker is. She will find that one first, I think, tonight when
she reads a few pages before going to sleep. In the pocket of her
favorite white jacket. I hide one in the box of porridge in the
kitchen cupboard, in the pre-Columbian pot on the windowsill,
one under the mattress and one in her sewing machine case. I
hide the notes in increasingly obscure places so that some will
be found within days, others weeks or months, and some not for
years. A few I put in places so obscure that the notes might go
with her should she ever move. These could be found one day in
a new home where I myself have never been. Then I sit.

I sit quietly in the living room on the couch that has been my bed. I close my eyes and for some time I concentrate on not thinking. I focus all my attention on the breath passing in and out of my nostrils and soon I begin to sense small beads of energy flowing down my arms. The beads are like tiny pin-points of light that flow, uninterrupted, down my arms and out the tips of my fingers. They swirl through the flat, twirling and diving until they have filled all the rooms—until they have found all the notes. The notes become part of the swirl of light that radiates as a pinwheel with me at the center and it becomes impossible to know any more which way the flow of energy is going. Soon I open my eyes. I am late.

Quickly I gather my things and wash my face. For one more long minute I stand by the door trying to pierce this room with my eyes. Then I pick up my bags and leave. In the cab, I choose not to talk. Instead I soak up King's Cross, Darlinghurst Road; I watch one of the white cockatoos on the edge of the Domain, twisting my neck to keep it in view for as long as I can, the Art Gallery, the gum trees.

I imprint these things on my brain and I think of the friend I am leaving. I lean back in the cab and tell myself that I will be back.

*   *   *   *   *

This is what I think. If there is any way to make a simple thing complicated, it can be done in New Zealand. "Why," I say, "are sixty people coming to the ceremony? Sixty people will not fit in this tiny room with all these artifacts and all these crates."

"Sixty people are coming," he says, "because there are sixty people who need to be invited." This is very Maori.

Here is what I know: the only way to get something done in a hurry in New Zealand is to leave the country. "Does the ceremony," I say, "*have* to be held in the room with the artifacts? Can we not use the empty gallery upstairs that will hold sixty people?"

"The ceremony," he says patiently, "must be held in the room with the objects because the ceremony is to bless the objects."

"Can we not," I say, "take a small selection of objects upstairs to the empty gallery and let them represent all the objects?" This I say, knowing that it is a bad idea. This I say, knowing that the objects should not be carried upstairs and that there is not enough security upstairs and that there is no climate control upstairs. This I say, also knowing that this man will not budge.

"Done," he says.

"That is fine," I say, "and you must be here by 3:00 at the latest to choose the objects that will be taken upstairs. I will try to unpack as many as I can by then so you will have enough to select from. The crew goes home at 4:00 and there will be no one to carry them up after that, so it is important that you be here by 3:00." I say this as if I believe that he will be there and he says, "Fine," as if he also believes that he will be there. This is very Maori.

At 3:00 he is not there. At 3:30 he is not there and I am still in blue jeans and must go back to the hotel to change because at 5:30 the elders and the Mayor and the guests will arrive for the ceremony. At 4:15 he is not there and I appoint myself a Maori. I choose this object because it is large, that one because it is small, those two because they are made of stone and the other because it is whalebone. Some I choose because they are pretty and others because they are not and the crew has gone home. I carry the objects up the stairs by myself to the big tables that have been set up in the empty gallery along with sixty chairs. At 4:45 he is not there and I appoint myself designer. I place that object towards the rear and this towards the front; the other at an angle. I tell the guard he will die a miserable death if he leaves this room even long enough to pee, and I leap in the car. I get lost on the way to my hotel.

There is no time for a shower so I wash my face and change to a skirt that has not been properly ironed and stockings and heels and a blouse that has not been properly ironed and I get lost on the way back from my hotel.

When I get back to the gallery there is no longer any place to park the car so I park very far away and run, in my heels, until I get to the door. I pause for a moment, take a deep breath, and then, looking poised and cheerful I sweep in the door.

The man who was to be there at 3:00 is there. He smiles and kisses me on the cheek. He tells me he has already been in the room and compliments me on what a lovely selection I have made. This is very Maori.

I smile and thank him for the compliment and think that I might just have to kill him. This is very American.

＊　　　　＊　　　　＊　　　　＊　　　　＊

April 20, 1984, Auckland, N.Z.
The American Federation of Arts
New York, U.S.A.

Hi, Guys!

Things have been wild this first week. I nearly had a nervous breakdown yesterday between the film crews (two of them!); adjusting to the personalities at the Gallery and the Museum; racing back and forth across town from the Gallery to the Museum making sure all objects were present and accounted for in one location or the other, and preparing for the ceremony last night—all before this entire country shut down for Easter, which it did last night. Last but not least is that the climate control system at the Gallery malfunctioned at about noon yesterday—the day before a four-day holiday weekend. Within two hours the humidity in the Te Maori room had dropped to 48%, about 7% lower than it should be, only 3% above the absolute minimum to which we are bound by our contract with the New Zealand Government, the lending museums, the entire Maori population of New Zealand, and her Majesty the Queen! It was falling fast.

Within an hour I'd located three electric fans and several pans of water and set them all over the floor in a last-ditch effort to boost the humidity. It worked. The hygrothermograph began to creep up. (It's like knowing CPR and finally having to use it! I can now say that old trick has been tried and that it works.) But this gets even better. The reason the air system was out, they said, was because of a minor flood in the room directly above us! I freaked out. The Maori objects (whatever I've unpacked from the temporary packing so far) were spread all over the floor on foam rubber because the room is so small and there are no tables. In the meantime, people were about to arrive for the ceremony. Peta was supposed to show up at 3:00 to make a selection of objects but he was held up at a meeting and never got there. I appointed myself Maori-for-a-Day and picked them myself, hauled them upstairs by myself. The indemnity board would *die,* but there was no way out. They probably all mysteriously broke out in hives that day and can't figure out why.

When it was all over and everyone else had gone home I got one of the conservators to come and help. We found tables and set them up in the Te Maori room, carried all the things from the ceremony back downstairs, got everything off the floor and onto tables or on top of crates and hoisted all the crates up onto chunks of two-by-four—in case the flood upstairs decided to come downstairs. I did all this wearing stockings and heels. We finished at about 10:00 P.M.

The ceremony was quite a scene. At one point there was a bit of fussing and commotion in the front row of elders. They would not speak because the Mayor of Auckland had just made a welcoming speech and the Mayor of Auckland just happens to be a woman! Finally a few elders, apparently ones from more liberal tribal groups, did get up and speak, but several absolutely refused. I'd cordoned off the tables where the objects were spread out at the ceremony, but at the end all sixty people stood up and swarmed right over the rope and started ooh-ing and ah-ing and picking everything up! Laurence Mann, the

Director of the Museum, winked at me and said, "And how are your underwriters feeling right now?"

"They're a little nervous," I said, hovering at the edge of the mob, waiting for a crash. The registrar's manual does not explain how to tell a Maori elder he can no longer pick up *his* sacred ancestor because it (he!) is now on *your* government's insurance policy. This time *I* nearly broke out in hives, which means the indemnity board must have had a collective stroke in absentia.

So now it's the weekend and phase one is past, for better or worse. Next week I'll face the fact that we just do not fit in that room to pack the show with all the objects, all the temporary crates, all the final travel crates, four people and all our tools. I don't think Sam is very good with a saber saw when he's hanging by his toes from the ceiling.

Anyway, Peta is great, Lesley and Kevin are great and I'm having a *good time* this time, in spite of a few minor (!!!!) problems. The elders said a special prayer for me at the ceremony last night. They kinda thought I might need it. I kinda think so, too.

Love,
Carol

April 26, 1984, Auckland, N.Z.
The American Federation of Arts
New York, U.S.A.

Dear Friends,

Today I got to inspect the first of 174 objects. This is Thursday of the second week here. So much for the best laid plans. It was my intention to have everything inspected and neatly grouped next to its appointed crate by the time Sam arrived (this Sunday) and instead I've been chasing floods, film crews, dwindling humidity, Maori elders, Easter holidays, a room too small and a show too big. Today was the first day that order began to emerge from the chaos. I unpacked the last object from its temporary crate, threw out 472 tons of used bubble wrap, swept the floor and sat down to survey the scene. Maybe there will be a show after all.

There is one more wiggle in the plot before we can begin to roll. In order to make the proper crate groupings we have to move fifteen objects at the Gallery up to the Museum, and thirty-one objects from the Museum down to the Gallery—of course several of the crates that were delivered to the Gallery now belong at the Museum and several the other way around— so I've reserved a two-ton truck for Monday because all this stuff is bloody huge and today we spent all day sorting and temporarily repacking what I had just finished unpacking, and, well . . . you see what I mean?

Anyway, life is going well. My little hotel unit has become quite homelike. (I can't move in with Lesley and Kevin for another week because his parents are in town for Easter.) It has a kitchen which I've stocked with various things and the hotel supplies a limited range of pots, pans and utensils. No one steals them. Can you believe it?

I've eaten only two meals out since I got here.

Lesley assured me they'll show me some good restaurants real soon but I'm actually quite happy shopping and cooking for myself. The trick is that New Zealand closes at 5:00 or 5:30— all of it. That means you vault out the door from work, hurl your body into the car and slide, screaming, into the produce market as they're rolling down the gate. Then you throw them a handful of money and barrel across the street into the butcher shop or fish store. No one supplies bags here. They wrap things in little paper parcels instead, so by the time you get back to the car you look like a family juggling act with a veal chop in one hand, two lemons in the other, a packet of silver beet arcing over your head and all manner of things lying on the ground around your feet while you try to find the car keys.

I would like to remind all of you that you can write to me too this time since I will be in one place long enough to get mail for a change . . .

Lesley:

"Oh dear, what have they done now?"

"You're going to love this story. Peta tells me the local elders here in Auckland contacted the museum and said they had to come and remove five chips from one of the objects. It's an enormous storage house front, a very important object historically and is insured for over five million dollars."

"And they want to take chips off it?"

"Very good. You're a podiatrist and you noticed something was wrong with that idea, straight off. Imagine what it could do to a registrar?! Anyway, since the museums own these things in trust for the Maori people you can't really refuse them. They said one chip was to be buried on the grounds of the Auckland Museum, one on the grounds of the Metropolitan Museum in New York, one in St. Louis, one in San Francisco, and the final one to be crumbled into the sea in New Zealand when the exhibition returns. This is to carry the spirit of the exhibition safely home."

"This is great. Have you . . ."

"Wait, there's more! Apparently, two Maori carvers arrived on the appointed day and were met by two conservators with a scalpel. 'Don't bother,' says one of the carvers, 'I have a chisel.' And he proceeds to pull one out of his pocket and shave five large splinters off the back of the piece."

"It was nice of him to do it on the back, wasn't it?"

"Yes, I thought so too. This all happened before I arrived, thank God, so I didn't have to undergo a nervous breakdown worrying about the ramifications of this act on our insurance policy. The US Government Indemnity program is going to get a real run for its money with this show. The carver wrapped the splinters in a little cloth and flax parcel and they have been given to me to safeguard throughout the tour. I think I will have the parcel grafted onto my skin so I can sleep nights for the next eighteen months. Maybe I get crumbled into the sea if I lose this thing!"

"Have you prepared them for this in New York?"

"Yes, I wrote to Douglas at the Met and told him to start digging a hole on the grounds."

April 28, 1984, Auckland, N.Z.
The American Federation of Arts
New York, U.S.A.

Dear Friends,

I just had to send this brief note to make you green with envy. This weekend I went out to a place on the coast west of Auckland. A few people from the Gallery have places in a small community there. It is very raw and wild, with towering volcanic cliffs. We hiked for hours and hours along the sides of these cliffs like mountain goats, sometimes waiting for breaks in the crashing waves so we could scurry across the rocks. Once, I miscalculated and ended up out in the middle, clinging to a tiny outcropping of rock while a wave came in. I did not get swept out to sea, although things looked a bit dicey for a minute there.

There's an ancient Maori cave, a cavern formed thousands of years ago by a volcanic blow-out, it seems. It's high up on the side of a mountain facing inland, and on Sunday I climbed up there by myself. I sat in the mouth of the cave in the sun for more than an hour and had a little think. You can see a waterfall from there. In the afternoon, Sam and I collected shells on the beach and then we all sat around a huge bonfire with mugs of gunpowder tea and plates of Welsh rarebit on crusty bread (I'm the cook of course). There are hardly any other people out there except the few who have houses on that tiny dirt road. It's a good thing I just got my new ten-year passport before I left home. I may not come back until it expires. Please dust my desk off from time to time—you know how all that soot can blow in the window and accumulate.

I'm off to get my laundry out now. I've run up and down five flights of stairs seven times in the course of this short letter since the washer and dryer have about a four-minute cycle. I gave my laundry to the hotel to do once and I think they put it through the juicer. I was lucky my shirts still had sleeves. They certainly had no buttons.

Love,
Carol

*   *   *   *   *

It is best in the morning. There is no one else there. At that time it is possible to stand at the very edge of the sea. The world is uninterrupted; planes of liquid and vapor, blue and turquoise and brown sweeping away from each other with a hugeness that steals the breath. A lone white bird flies by very slowly.

I move only with great caution. The fear is that abruptness will shatter the fragile balance of a world in which only this place and I exist. To the left and right stretches the beach. The sand is creamy, smooth, and is etched with such elegance. A tongue has twirled languidly through this softness, leaving rounded, swirling trails. To the left there is also a rock. It juts from the waves, a huge pyramid a hundred yards offshore. It is fierce and stands watch. My toes disappear in the sand.

It is easy to think this is all—there could not possibly be more of the world than can be seen at this moment. But the cliffs are too strong. Slowly, and with great care, I turn to face them. They shoot into the sky, black and vertical, jagged and gouged by centuries. The cliffs lean over the beach and only a few of the bravest small trees cling to their face. These cliffs do not move, their rocks and crumbled edges having been set long ago in molten lava and cooled, capturing forever the same expression they wore when first they burst from the sea. They do not swirl and shift with promise as does the sand. They preserve.

I must prepare myself each time, by first watching the gentler faces of the sea and the sky to the west. From them I draw strength until finally I am able to turn and face the cliffs. Then I hear a thousand years of laughter and a thousand more of tears, see a thousand births and a thousand deaths in the pitted faces that tower over me.

Were it not for the strength that I have found in the sea and sky I would have to run away into the ocean, soar up into the clouds—anything to escape the voice of these cliffs. It deafens. It gives more than you want to know and asks more than you care to tell. Soon the voices let me go. I turn, exhausted, elated, and begin to walk north along the beach.

There are some people now, I note with relief. A few adults and two children, so far down the beach that at times they vaporize, disappearing into the dancing light. They are dots of blue and red, a bit of yellow, and strangely, it is only the small voices of the children that carry. Perhaps these voices are lighter, caught by the breeze before they've had a chance to become encumbered by years. I tell myself I will come back always to this place. I say it belongs to me. But I need not have said it—I too have been preserved in the pitted faces of the cliffs and the truth is that I now belong to this place.

Soon I tear myself away and start back up the gravel road. There will be tea at the house.

*   *   *   *   *

May 2, 1984, Auckland, N.Z.

The American Federation of Arts
New York, U.S.A.

Hi, Guys,

I am now moved into Lesley and Kevin's and have finally gotten to unpack for the first time. That is a nice feeling. It's good here. My part of the house is quite separate, but I'm finding it fascinating trying to adjust to this business of living with other people around. Living alone can get to be a real habit!

By the way, thank you for your phone calls at five and six a.m. that sent three adults and one child leaping through the ceiling. Maybe we'll all get better at calculating the time difference eventually.

You should see our little packing crew at work. Get this scene: Brian looks like a character out of Dickens. He is tall and skinny, with long hair that he wears pulled back in a ponytail. He's got very thin features, a wonderful hawkish nose, and wears a big lock of hair in front of each ear like sideburns. Sometimes, for whatever reason, he tucks his pants into his knee socks so it looks as if he's wearing knickers. Gavin is tall and willowy. He has a punk haircut, wears dark glasses all the time, indoors and out, and wears only black clothes. He arrives at work on a motorcycle. Sam is a shy, quiet Italian-American from New York. He wears heavy American-made work shoes and industrial-looking light blue shirts with the name of his company across the back. He is about 50 and the rest of us are in our thirties. I look sort of wholesome, with barrettes in my hair and a scrubbed face, but also with overalls and a sweatshirt—a sort of Alice in Wonderland in truck driver drag.

We finished the first crate today and went out for a beer after work to celebrate. From the looks we got, I figure people thought we were some bizarre new rock band, maybe a combination of Lawrence Welk and the Rolling Stones. Actually, though, it was very much like when I'm couriering a show: the sight of me in a truck stop with two truck drivers always has people scratching their heads. It's very funny.

Things may finally get rolling now. It took eleven men to carry the *empty* crate for the Pukeroa gateway up the steps of the museum. Painful place, that museum. Everything is up or down tiny flights of stairs—three steps here, five there. They have no four-wheeled furniture dollies and no real crew since there are few changing exhibitions here. We gathered conservators, librarians, cooks, janitors and curators to haul that crate in. Wait till we fill it! (Actually, I'll be hiring outside movers to carry it back out.)

You will be pleased to know that a conservator here has done us a great favor. The main figure on one ridgepole in the exhibition had its penis broken off many years ago. The museum director at that time, I am told, threw the penis out (!) because he thought it was obscene. (This will give you some sense of what conservation practices have been in this country. They *are* changing, though.) Anyway, a conservator here made the carving a new penis. I think for diplomacy's sake (he is obviously very proud of his handiwork) we should wait until everything arrives in New York and then telex down for permission to castrate it again.

It's gotten pretty chilly here and to them it's winter. For us, it's about like early fall. Some sun, some rain, some wind and temperatures somewhere between 50 and 70 degrees. Not bad, really. The houses are generally unheated and have maybe a fireplace or a few space heaters for nights when it gets cold enough to need them. I couldn't figure out why I was complaining about the cold so much, but it finally occurs to me—I'm not used to it being this cold *inside* the house. Fifty degrees outside is nothing, but fifty degrees in my bedroom when I'm trying to sleep, I am not used to, considering the way we overheat everything at home. Lesley has donated one of the space heaters specifically to this poor, pampered American.

I'll write soon . . .

Love,
Carol

Lesley:

"What do you mean, he made it a new one!?"

"Just what I said. I kept looking around at all the objects in the room and back to this one, thinking, 'something's wrong.'

The conservator noticed me looking. 'I made it a new . . . uh . . .' 'Oh, of course,' I say, 'so you did,' meanwhile thinking, 'My God, what are we going to do? It looks like a cucumber!' "

"What did he make this thing out of?"

"Plastic wood, I guess. Then he painted it to match the color of the old wood. This is what I call the 'auto body' school of conservation—you know, if the piece loses a nose, you make it a new nose! It doesn't go on so much in the States anymore. It used to be standard practice, and the test of how good a conservator you were was how cleverly you could make the new part look like the old. I've even seen people drill fake insect holes in things to match the ones all over the original."

"Well, what would you do instead?"

"Now the generally accepted idea is that you shouldn't deceive the viewer into thinking they're looking at an authentic example of the way a Maori 500 years ago would have carved a penis, when in fact they are looking at the way a conservator in 1984 imagines a Maori 500 years ago would have carved a penis. Now conservators would stabilize the damage if there was any chance it might continue to deteriorate. In terms of cosmetic work they would tone in the broken edge with some watercolor if the raw break were really distracting—which I admit, it was."

"So are you going to castrate it again?"

"Not me, kiddo! This conservator is very pleased with himself."

May 5, 1984, Auckland, N.Z.

The American Federation of Arts
New York, U.S.A.

Hi,

Well, this past week at work was pretty mucked up. All along, I've known that Air New Zealand was dead wrong about the aircraft they assigned to this show, but the trick was getting them to "discover" it themselves. (After all, I'm just a "girl," so why should they believe me?) I hate diplomacy! What I really wanted to say was, "Look you fools, stop reassuring me that it will fit, because I know it won't." You'd have been proud of me, though; I didn't say that. After turning myself inside out with sweetness I finally figured out a way to effect this brilliant realization on their part. You should have seen their faces when they finally looked at each other, then looked at me, and said, aghast, "It's not going to fit on those planes!" (I couldn't control a mildly hysterical laugh, but otherwise remained quite cool.) Pandemonium reigns. It's panic in River City. Apparently, when they agreed to sponsor the exhibition by providing free transportation, they didn't quite focus on what it was they were committing themselves to. I don't know how it happened. I sent them a list of crates almost a year ago and since the crates didn't exist at that time I even padded all the dimensions by about ten inches just in case. It is my suspicion that the list I sent them never made its way from the executives to the cargo personnel who would actually be the ones to load the planes. Anyway, I'd hate to think we've built a boat in the basement and now can't get it out. But don't panic (there's enough panic down here. We don't need any more from New York), we're working on it.

Besides that little fly in the ointment, late Friday afternoon at the end of week one, I looked at Sam, Brian and Gavin and said, "Well, guys, we've done two and a half crates in one week. Air New Zealand plans to move us out the week of June 4th, which means we've got three more weeks and 23 1/2 more crates. What do you think?" Sam—calm, quiet Sam who is always the one reassuring me, always the one saying, "Don't worry, it will go faster than you think now that we're rolling"—that very same Sam looks me square in the eye and says, "It can't be done."

So I went charging to the phone to tell Air New Zealand to make it more like the week of June 11th, which was the original plan I'd drifted away from before leaving New York because it seemed like too much time for packing. It is not too much time! We'll be lucky if we finish without working nights. Fortunately, everyone gets along well and is maintaining their sense of humor as we haul, sweat, lift, cut and juggle.

I'll keep you informed,
Carol

May 10, 1984, Auckland, N.Z.
The American Federation of Arts
New York, U.S.A.

Dear everyone,

It is 8:30 P.M. and I'm in bed already. We've started working late some days now because it's become clear that we just won't make it. Even Sam is starting to show the strain a bit, and now I'm the one trying to reassure him.

This week I abandoned all attempts at tact and diplomacy, announced that L was turning back into a New Yorker, and proceeded to get things done. I turned to Brian and coolly said, "What does it take in this country to get a lumber order we've been waiting for for two weeks? Does it take more money? We'll pay more money. Does it take me renting a truck to go pick it up myself? I'll rent a truck." Brian kept interrupting throughout my monologue, trying to explain how the lumber yard had had a problem with their saw or something like that, but I wouldn't let him talk. "Don't explain!" I said. "Just get the goddamned lumber here by 9:00 tomorrow morning and don't tell me how you did it!" The lumber arrived at 9:00 the next morning. Poor Brian. It's a good thing we've become great friends or he might kill me.

I also managed a bit of a triumph with Air New Zealand, if I do say so myself. Working with their cargo personnel we finally figured out how to get the crates on the planes—they have to enter at the widest part of the plane rather than at floor level, the way pallets usually roll through cargo doors. This means that these enormous and heavy crates must be placed on top of stacks of old lumber to raise them up approximately thirty-two inches, so that they are at the wide part of the plane's belly. Even at that, if all our calculations are correct, we will clear by only half an inch on either side and an inch on top!

Anyway, that turned out to be the easy part. I'd been working with the cargo people, but now the executives called me at the museum to say there were some very serious problems and that I must come in to meet with them. The meeting lasted two hours, began with three severe-looking executives glaring and snarling at me ("What arrangements," one says, "have you made from Los Angeles to New York?" "None," says I, "you will be writing a through air waybill to New York." "Absolutely not!" he says. "Our responsibility ends when it arrives at our terminal in L.A." "And what," sneers another, "did you think you would do when the couriers have to go off to clear customs in Honolulu? How are they going to stay with the shipments then?" "You," I say, "are going to get tarmac clearance for our agent in Honolulu to go planeside and take over supervision while the couriers go through customs," and ended with them ready to roll a velvet carpet down the runway). I have to say, it was brilliant, and when I get home I'll tell you what I did. It was not exactly standard diplomatic practice, but seems to have done the trick.

Love,
Carol

*   *   *   *   *

In the closet there are skirts. There is even a dress. I stare at them blankly, scratching absently at my hip. The neat line of clothes, I think, should have some meaning and doesn't. My eyes are drawn to the left and down. There is a small pile there on the floor in the corner. These are dirty clothes from the last week. This is my laundry. I stop scratching now and stare for a moment, still blankly, but with the growing knowledge that here there is some meaning. With effort I bring my eyes back to the skirts in the closet. I know I should choose one. This will be an important meeting. A great deal depends on the outcome of this meeting.

"I'm sure you are aware that there are serious problems," these men have said. "You must come for a meeting on Wednesday morning." I have not met these men, but even on the phone I can tell that they are wearing dark suits and white shirts. Even on the phone I can tell that they are much older than I.

My eyes are drawn once again to the laundry pile. This time I begin to move. On the top is a pair of jeans. They are rumpled. They have been in this pile on the floor since Monday, but I pull them on. One last time I look back at the clothes hanging in the closet and now, with greater conviction, turn and continue to dress. The jeans are a bit too short. I have never noticed this before. There is a sweatshirt. It is a brown sweatshirt that I have had since I was twelve years old. There is a small hole on the left shoulder and now there is also an oil stain on the chest. I put it on.

I am moving carefully, methodically, and I am working very hard not to hear the voices in my head. "They will judge you for this," says one. "They will think you are a child," says another, and a third says, "No, they will discover that you really *are* a child."

A navy blue bandana has drifted out of the laundry pile and under the nightstand. I get down on my knees to pull it out. It is one that I bought at a truck stop in Arizona years ago and is very faded and worn. I tie it around my neck. "This is ridiculous," a voice says. "If this doesn't work you will lose the support of these people and of this airline. The exhibition will fall through because there is no longer the time or the money to find alternatives." "It will be your fault if this happens," accuses another voice. I wonder how many of them there can be, these voices in my head. They are all different and all scolding and clamoring at me.

Next I put on the socks. They are wild cotton socks with horizontal stripes of red, green, purple and blue. They are already stretched out, and crumple immediately to my ankles. I put on my running shoes and tie them. They are very dirty. It was raining and muddy yesterday. Now I go out to the car. There is a light frost on the windshield.

I begin to drive down the road and the first wave of fear rolls over me. "What are you doing!?" my mind screams. "You can't go to a critical meeting looking like this! Jane would not go to a critical meeting dressed like this!" I push it down and keep driving. I am cold with sweat. Strength returns as I pull out into the traffic on Shore Road and head for downtown. Carefully and with great concentration I keep myself from thinking of what I am going to say at this meeting. I do not think of what they might say to me and how I might respond. I turn on the radio, loud, and sing with Billy Idol. Diligently I work at not having the meeting before the meeting.

The second wave of fear hits when I find a parking space in front of the office building. "Now you've blown it," the voices shriek. "There is no time to go home and change. They will take you for the fool that you are!" The voices are wild now, screaming and jeering at me. I am paralyzed, sitting in the parking space, staring out the windshield. I do not look down at myself. If I do not look down I can still pretend that this is a dream, that I am really wearing my trim black skirt and a white blouse. I pretend I have pearls on. I get out of the car and sling my sack over a shoulder. I lock the doors, and as I am doing this, catch a glimpse of my muddy shoes. I go through the revolving door. It is not a dream.

The elevator on the way to the eighteenth floor is crowded. They are all men and they are all wearing dark suits. They are all older than I. The men in the elevator pretend they are not looking at me. I pretend that people who look like me ride in this elevator all the time, and somewhere between the ground and the eighteenth floor I dress myself. Carefully, I clothe myself in the fact that I know my business very well. I dress myself in the years of experience that have placed me in this elevator.

I am different by the time I reach the eighteenth floor. I move with certainty now, walking up to the receptionist. I am aware of how fragile are these clothes that I wear. The only thing that qualifies me to meet with these men, to argue with them, to discuss anything with them, is the fact that I know something. I have no other armor.

The receptionist peers down her nose at me. She cannot see these invisible clothes and for a moment the fragile garments quiver and seem about to unravel. She thinks I am making a delivery. I pull my cloak back around me. "Matthew Newley," I say clearly, as if I am wearing my trim black skirt and white blouse. "I have an appointment at 9:00." Her expression changes. She talks into the intercom on her desk, still looking at me, and is told to bring me in. She leads, and by the time we reach the door, I have forgotten this receptionist who still thinks maybe I am making a delivery. I sweep into the room grinning.

There are three of them. One is sitting behind a large desk and the others next to it. I can see by the way their hands are placed on the desk and the arms of the chairs that they have planned to stand up. They have intended to stand, as is only proper they should when a lady enters the room. But they do not stand and they do not even notice that they have not stood. I am at the desk now. My hand is out and I am shaking hands, saying good morning, moving quickly and broadly. I am filling the room. I whirl around and flop into the chair that has been placed for me, facing the desk. I cross my legs. The leg of my jeans hikes up even higher now and the striped sock is rolled around my ankle. I relax. I smile and wait for them to speak.

There is no sound. For an incredibly long moment there is silence and I grow stronger in the silence because I know that already, before a word is spoken, it has worked. This thing that I have done without quite knowing why, has had its effect. In the silence I know that while I sang with Billy Idol, they have had the meeting before the meeting. They knew that I would be a woman executive from New York and that I would come in and tell them how to run their airline. They knew this and they knew also exactly who they were and who they wanted to be in relation to a woman executive from New York. While I sang with Billy Idol they imagined they had heard me speak and were smugly pleased by their own response.

The three men in dark suits stare at me. It is at this moment that I clear my throat and begin the meeting.

*   *   *   *   *

May 14, 1984, Auckland, N.Z.

The American Federation of Arts
New York, U.S.A.

Hi, Folks,

Air New Zealand is still jumping through hoops to be nice and help us out. I think I've got them terrified. That's real good.

The social event of my life took place on Saturday. Brian got married on his "farm" on Waiheke Island—a two-hour ferry ride from Auckland. The reason I put farm in quotes is that there really is no farm yet. There is a flock of sheep, three outhouses they slapped together for the occasion, the beginnings of a barn, and the bush (forest, to us). It was fabulous!

I have to admit, it's getting harder and harder to think about coming back to New York. This place has made me remember that I'm a country kid at heart. Besides, I feel as if I live here now. I have a home, a family (I've long since gotten over the awkwardness of living with people and have come to love living with Lesley and Kevin. I even enjoy their four-year-old, James), a job, a routine. I have colleagues and friends; and the very idea that in a few weeks I will just get up and leave . . . well, I can hardly think about it.

Don't get nervous. I am, of course, coming home and will surely get right back into things as soon as I'm there.

Brian has also invited me out to his farm my last weekend here to help shear and muster his flock of sheep. (Sorry—you have to muster 'em before you can shear 'em.) Mustering means *finding* the little suckers out in the fields and scaring the daylights out of them until they run into this paddock where you jump on them and shear the wool off their backs to make

sweaters for people who live in cold places. I can't wait. There
will be nothing but sheep and sea and bush and sleeping bags
and being dirty and probably freezing cold. Sounds delicious.
New York City it ain't!

See you soon?

Love,

Carol

Lesley:

"You're not looking all that chipper today. Was it a bad day at
work?"

"I don't know what it is about this place. You know I never
used to cry? I can't remember when I last cried . . . Before I
came to New Zealand, that is. Now it seems I started weeping
when I left here in 1982 and haven't stopped since."

"I guess you're making up for lost time."

"I must be. I'm getting a little nervous, that's all. Do you
realize that in about three weeks I am actually leaving here?"

"It will be hard, but you'll be back, you know."

"It's not only that. It's not only leaving all my friends here and
all the things I've come to love about this country. That will be
excruciating, but it is also that I am finally about to take these
things out of here. There's been no time to think about it up until
now. I've been completely crazed with lumber and airplanes,
customs permits, saws that don't work, and so on and so on.
Lesley! I'm about to take Uenuku out of this country for the first
time!"

"Is there anyone you can talk to about it if you're worried?"

"Well, Peta is coming up to Auckland in a week or so, and I
thought I'd see if he had a reassuring word or two. There's also a
Maori Anglican minister I've been meaning to look up. The
New Zealand Vice Consul in New York gave me his name. I
think it's time to call him and get my 'mana' put in order, if you
know what I mean."

"It can't hurt."

May 25, 1984, Auckland, N.Z.
The American Federation of Arts
New York, U.S.A.

Dear everyone,

Things are drawing to a close. The closer we get to departure, the crazier things get. There have to be at least a million details still floating around that need to be pinned down.

Here's one detail you'll love: I had New Zealand Express send the head of their "Heavy Gang" up to the museum the other day. This is a team that is trained to move safes and heavy equipment by hand. The guy that showed up was not all that tall, but had a neck like a tree trunk. His shoulders and arms were so massive that I don't think he could have scratched his left shoulder with his right hand—he couldn't reach over that far. His name was Jimmy. I pointed to the Pukeroa Gateway crate and said, "How many people will we need to carry that out of the building when we go?" He doesn't talk, he just strolls over to it and gets a hand under one end. He gives a little hoist— not actually lifting it, of course, just getting a feel for it. He stands up and looks at me. "Eight," he says. I laugh. "No, no," I say. "Don't try to save us money. You can't possibly lift this crate with only eight men. It weighs nearly 1800 pounds!" "Eight," he says. Now I look at him a little skeptically because I realize he is not making a joke. "Look," I say, "I'll take your word on this if you say it's enough, but do you know what we're carrying? We can take no risks." "Eight men," he says. "OK, Jimmy. Reserve eight men."

I can't wait to see this!

I'm estimating it will take about two weeks for us to unpack and inspect the whole show when it gets to the Met, so don't count on my presence in the office till after that. (I will, of course, come in to say hi!)

Love,
Carol

Telex: June 1, 1984

Attn: Carol O'Biso, Gallery Auckland

Critical we know final contents of each shipment to prepare customs entry papers. Cn u supply immediately?

Best regards,

Ellie Cole, Barthco, Phila.

Telex: June 1, 1984

Attn: Ellie Cole or Bill Evans, Barthco, Phila.

Still frantically trying to make all small objects fit into three crates allotted to them. Final list available tomorrow with luck. Am aware of urgency. Also trying to wrench air waybill numbers for 3 shipments out of ANZ. Will supply ASAP.

Desperately,

Carol O'Biso, Gallery Auckland.

Lesley:

"Are you serious?"

"Yes. I can't believe I never made a connection, but we have had two blackouts and one false alarm fire at the gallery in the past week! Everyone there is freaking out that so many things could go wrong in one week!"

"I'd freak out, too."

"Only yesterday did I realize that we're leaving next week!"

"What's next, I wonder?"

"I don't know, but the ancestors had better cut it out if they're the ones causing the trouble. We'll never finish packing with all these interruptions."

"Did you call the Maori Anglican minister?"

"Yes, I made a date to have lunch with him tomorrow."

Telex: June 3, 1984

Attn: Ellie Cole or Bill Evans, Barthco, Phila.

Urgent

Here is an adjustment to final (we thought) box list telexed yesterday: Move number 20 from box 22 to box 24 and delete one of the number 77s from box 24.

Sorry.

Carol O'Biso, Gallery Auckland

Telex: June 5, 1984

Urgent attn: Ellie Cole or Bill Evans, Barthco, Phila.

Sure you are enjoying this as much as I am but here is one more revision of contents of boxes 22, 23 and 24.

Box 22 contains numbers:

4, 171, 14, 160, 149, 62, 97, 98, 20, 158, 162, 161, 157, 31, 107, 168, 32, 148, 39, 48, 165, 10, 17, 1, 58, 166, 13, 174, 111, 114, 29, 116, 105, 117, 102, 37, 141, 59, 95, 51, 82.

Box 23 contains numbers:

172, 12, 96, 167, 22, 120, 146, 140, 41, 139, 2, 122, 80, 110, 118, 115, 81, 52, 103, 40, 16, 115.

Box 24 contains numbers:

132, 93, 25, 3, 26, 24, 145, 11, 108, 49, 34, 35, 138, 125, 137, 56, 23, 44, 144, 183, 106, 45, 170, 21, 18, 147, 27, 73, 94, 19, 104, 77, 76, 74, 75, 78, 159.

This is final.

At last . . . AWB # for shipment one is 086/6155 5115

shipment two, 086/6155 5104

shipment three, 086/6155 5093

Best regards,

Carol O'Biso, Gallery Auckland

Telex: June 5, 1984

Attn: Ellie Cole or Bill Evans, Barthco, Phila.

Oops! Please include number 15 in box 22 and delete one of the 115s in box 23 and make it 109. Things aren't going the way we planned.

Sorry again. This is final. (Really.)

Carol O'Biso, Gallery Auckland

Lesley:

"So what did the minister have to say? Did he get your mana in order?"

"It was a wonderful meeting. Very casual. Just talking while he made chicken soup in the kitchen. It's funny, nothing really specific was said, but I came out of it feeling tremendously relieved. I told him how concerned I was about taking these things out of the country. I think he was a little surprised at that . . ."

"I'll bet he was. After all, you're just a Pakeha."

"Yeah, us white folk aren't supposed to know anything about this sort of stuff. He said my heart seems to be in the right place, though, and it will probably be OK. No guarantees or anything—but probably OK."

"That doesn't sound all that reassuring to me."

"I know. Now that I'm telling it over, it doesn't sound it to me either, but at the time, it was. Listen to this, though. A very funny thing happened."

"Oh, good. You haven't had a funny story in a while."

"He was standing there cutting up broccoli while I leaned on the door jamb with a glass of wine. I mentioned something about what a hard time I had my first trip down here—how hard it was to get anything done. 'Yes,' he says, peering at me over his glasses. 'If we're being told what to do by an American, we move very slowly.' He starts cutting the celery and after a second or two looks up at me again. 'And if it's a woman,' he says, 'we move even more slowly than that.' Then he carefully scrapes all the cut up vegetables into the pot and finally looks at me over his glasses again. 'And if she's *white*?' he says, shaking his head, 'we hardly move at all.' "

"Well, bugger them!"

"Yes, exactly! I just hooted with laughter, stood there with my hands on my hips staring at this man in shock. 'Well, I didn't have a shot in hell did I?' I said. And he said 'Not a one.' "

"But you did it, didn't you?"

"Yes, now that you mention it, I did, didn't I?"

Peta:

"If this goes wrong I'll have to die, you know. Someone will have to die. The only payment could be a life."

Telex: June 7, 1984

Urgent attn: Carol O'Biso, Gallery Auckland

Hate to throw a monkey wrench in the gears of progress but cn u pls tell me in which box number 79 is packed? Need to know as we are finishing up papers on this shipment. If it isn't included in shipment 3 I shall weep.

Thx yr help. Looking forward to seeing you on the 15th.

Hang tough.

Ellie Cole, Barthco, Phila.

Telex: June 7, 1984

Attn: Ellie Cole, Barthco, Phila.

Ellie, don't weep. Number 79 is included in shipment 3. We are finished packing. No more changes. Bring champagne to JFK.

Carol O'Biso, Gallery Auckland

*   *   *   *   *

My friend has put her child to bed. She comes quietly down the stairs to my room where I am packing. I think of how long it will be before I see her again and I begin to cry. We talk and I laugh through my tears and cry through my laughter. We talk for a long time and then she hugs me and goes back upstairs. I crawl into bed. There, I fall into a wretched sleep, and in the night I have a dream about Uenuku.

It is a grey day and I see myself walking on the coast west of Auckland. I watch a plane cut through the low, scuttling clouds and hear its dull drone between the sound of the waves. The jagged cliffs, with their gnarled, pitted faces suddenly crumble. They collapse in grief, weep in anguish at the passing of this plane. I peer more closely.

With clear dream vision I see through the side of the plane, deep into its belly to a long wooden crate. I see through the walls of the crate and there lies Uenuku. He is comfortable in white flannel and foam rubber, but constricted. His head is carefully pillowed and his arms pinned at his sides. He is horizontal, as he was centuries ago when he led his people to this land, but now his crest points out and away. He smiles ruefully, patiently, at these well-meaning people. I watch him gaze sadly at the growing distance between him and the land and know that he will tolerate but not enjoy, he will permit but not condone, this going. The cliffs continue to weep until their tears fall around me like rain and I watch a sorrowful Uenuku leaving this land he has never before left.

He asks why we have done this, and looking deep inside me for an answer, I find none. The plane disappears in the distance and now I stand and dry my tears. I stand before Maori and Pakeha alike and tell of the pain and the anguish inside me. I tell how the ground shook when the wheels of this plane lifted off, for the land knew a loss so deep and unidentifiable that it shuddered in dread.

Then the light changes. It is a sunny day and it is January of 1986. I see myself walking, once again on this beach, and I am slightly older now. I hear the sound of a plane in the distance. Looking up and away I see that the plane is flying in this time, towards the land, and Uenuku's crest points homeward. The cliffs, too, notice the coming of this plane and they weep in joy. They applaud his return and their tears fall around me like rain until my upturned face runs wet with tears that are both theirs and mine.

I dry my tears. I stand once more before Maori and Pakeha, before all the people of the land. I stand quietly and with dignity. I say that it is done and that it is done well; he is weary now but very proud and he has led them home as promised. But I say also that it must never, never happen again because the risks are too grave. Then I begin to weep again. I weep and weep so that I think I will never stop. I stand by the towering cliffs, by the pounding sea, and my tears fall around them like rain.

Then I wake, twisted in damp, wrinkled sheets, and from my tormented mind comes the cry, "Oh, God, please let it be all right!"

FIVE

The Flower

When we landed in Honolulu I felt a little better. They were on American soil now. The deed was done and all we could do was go forward and do the best job possible. I no longer felt it was my responsibility to think of a way to stop it. It could no longer be stopped.

Here's how I knew I was back in the US. When we got to Los Angeles, the Air New Zealand crew at the cargo terminal asked if they could wait until half time to transfer the shipment to American Airlines. The L.A. Lakers were playing the Boston Celtics and the Lakers were ahead. I said it would be OK. We had plenty of time to make the transfer.

I called Gavin at the Gallery in Auckland to tell him where things had not gone according to plan and how to correct them. He would be leaving Auckland with the second shipment in only a matter of hours. The receptionist began transferring my call around the building to find him. I recognized each voice— Halina, Ed, Chris, Dean—I could imagine these people at their desks, on their phones. The call took me on a painful tour of a place in which I myself had been standing less than a day before. I wanted to call out to the voices and say, "It's me! It's me! Don't you know me?" But they could hear only the operator, "I have an overseas call for Mr. Johnson." I wondered what I was doing here instead of there.

It was 102 degrees when we landed in New York. Ellie Cole

and Bill Evans, our customs agents, were both there, and had brought me a cup of coffee. It was 6:00 A.M.—too early for champagne. "How long has it been like this?" I asked. "I don't remember this kind of heat in New York for ten years!" "A week," Bill said. "You missed the worst of it. They say it's finally going to cool down tomorrow." "Cool down to what?" I said. "Ninety-seven degrees?"

It took hours and hours for American to unload the plane and transfer our pallet to a tractor trailer. Because of the height of the truck we had to take a roundabout route through Long Island City—the least appealing way to enter Manhattan. In bumper-to-bumper traffic I watched the skyline slowly appear. At times it was almost invisible, vanishing briefly in the simmering white heat.

Never before had the sight of the New York skyline failed to fill me with a delightful feeling of being home. This is my city, a voice always said. This is where I belong. Now it said nothing, or I failed to hear it above the traffic noises. There was an appalling feeling of deadness. It's just the heat, I told myself.

If only it weren't so hot! I thought of Uenuku back in the truck and wondered if, with the same dream vision as I, he could see through the walls of his crate and through the walls of the truck. Could he see that we had taken him away from his rolling green hills to bring him to this?

When we got to the Metropolitan Museum, it took hours more while the riggers hoisted the enormous crates off the pallet one by one with a sling. Douglas Newton came down to the loading dock during this operation. "Congratulations," he said, giving me a kiss on the cheek. "You did it." I knew I should be pleased by the compliment. Instead I felt completely neutral about what I had done.

One by one the crates were wheeled through the building to the elevator and up to the Sackler balcony. Five of them, including the Pukeroa Gateway, did not fit in the elevator. "We'll have to 'carry'," said the museum registrar. "I'll arrange it for early next Monday morning and the five crates can stay in storeroom one until then." "Carry where?" I asked, incredulous. "Up the front steps from Fifth Avenue and in the main door," he said. "Then we carry up the grand staircase." "One of these crates," I said, "weighs 1700 or 1800 pounds!" "It won't be the first time," he replied.

Douglas helped me get my bags into a cab for the few short blocks to my apartment. I prayed not to run into any neighbors in the hall. "How was your trip?!" they'd say. "Welcome home. Did you have a good time?"

When I opened the apartment door I was stunned. A wall of heat hit me like a slap. The place was a furnace and looked strangely grimy. I showered, changed my clothes and took a cab to the AFA office.

For just a moment it seemed there was hope. It was such a thrill to see them all! Thank God, I thought. It's just that I'm tired. It's just that I've been up for more than two days. It will be fine. It will be normal, as soon as I've had some sleep.

Everyone gathered around. "How was it?" they said. "We loved your letters!" "How does it feel to be home?" "What do you think of this heat?" "We missed you." "I can't believe you actually did it!" "Wait till you see what's piled on your desk!"

Slowly, as they chattered on, the real reason for my distress rose thickly in the back of my throat. Yes, I was upset at the heat and the noise and the grime of New York, and yes, it had been hard to leave all my friends in New Zealand, but more than that, I suddenly knew that I was not proud of what I had done. I could not stand in front of these people with pride. Quietly, I began to tell the expectant faces about my ambivalence at being back. I told them also that I was not sure it was the right thing we had done, taking this exhibition out of the country. I told them I had come to see a little of what these objects meant to the Maori people.

Everyone had grown quiet because they had not heard me talk like this. My voice became low and strained with emotion and their embarrassment grew. As I spoke I was made stronger by finally having said these words. I stood boldly now before my colleagues and friends. I told them that it was a mistake and that I was not proud of my role in this taking, that there was no reason on earth good enough to justify having done this.

I stayed a few more minutes and talked of lighter things, of funny things, because their discomfort was extreme. Then I went home to my steamy apartment and cried.

Two days later I got up at 5:00 A.M. and went back to Kennedy Airport to meet Gavin arriving with the second shipment, and three days after that went back again to meet Brian with the third. All had gone well, and for the most part, according to plan.

On the Monday the riggers were going to "carry" we all gathered in the loading dock at the Met at 7:00 A.M. They started with the Pukeroa Gateway, the heaviest piece. They made the slow trek carefully, wheeling the crate from the loading dock up to Fifth Avenue and down along the sidewalk to 82nd Street, where it would be laid flat and carried up the main steps.

They started with twelve men; twelve of them in matching beige uniforms ringing the crate. They bent and tried to lift. It wouldn't even come off the sidewalk, so they tried with 18, and then 24, and finally 28 riggers, hip to hip, shoulder to shoulder around the crate. They hoisted and began to move like a centipede crawling slowly up to the first landing. Shuffling beige legs, matching black shoes. Soon we were inside and now came the worst. The grand staircase looked endless, disappearing into the heavens. I held my breath. They rested a moment at the foot and then it began. There was no sound except the grunting and shuffling. No sound but the struggle, and suddenly what had seemed like forever was over. They reached the top and set the crate down, letting out a collective sigh.

"You know," I said brightly, "that eight Maoris carried this crate in New Zealand?" The riggers were furious. They would not even speak to me. I had to admit, it was not the most diplomatic comment I had made in my life.

It took us almost a full two weeks to unpack and inspect the exhibition. During that time I started to feel a little better. For one thing, everything had arrived in perfect condition. The ancestors had made their first voyage without incident. Perhaps, like tiny babies, they were hardier than one would suspect by looking at them.

Jeanne Hedstrom, the exhibition's coordinator from AFA, came up to the Metropolitan while we were unpacking. "My God!" she said of the objects, "it's a forest of splinters!" It was true, but somehow the forest of splinters was holding its own.

The other reason I was feeling better was that I could still pretend. For at least two weeks I could pretend that nothing had changed, nothing was over. Brian and Gavin were in town. We spent all our time together when I wasn't working. Sam Martelli, our packer, had since returned to his home in Queens and he and his wife Lydia were planning a barbecue for us on the Fourth of July. So we were all together again; nothing had changed. Instead of being at the gallery in Auckland I was at the museum in New York. But I had brought Te Maori with me and some bits of Auckland as well. Everything was fine.

But the two weeks ended, of course. Brian and Gavin left on July 5. The exhibition was unpacked and thoroughly inspected and my work at the Metropolitan, until the installation, was reduced to visits two or three times a week to consult with the mount makers and conservators as they prepared the objects to be installed. I found myself back at AFA, back at my desk, back on the phone.

There were calls to make about frames for the upcoming Rothko exhibition, research to be done to ascertain why the lacquer was peeling on the Renaissance silver collection I had brought from London what seemed like years before but was only eight months. Suddenly, I was home. Suddenly, New Zealand had slipped through my fingers and disappeared. I found myself figuring out what time it was there, picturing everyone I knew and where they might be. Often I pictured Lesley and Kevin finding the tiny notes I had hidden in every corner of their house the day before I left.

Two days after Gavin and Brian headed home I had a phone call from Molly Wilson, the New Zealand Vice Consul who lived only a few blocks from my apartment. "I've just hung up the phone with Peta," she said. "He sends his love but there is something he asked me to tell you in person. Do you mind if I stop up for a few minutes?" As soon as I hung up there was a knot in my stomach. Only death is served up in quite this way, and I wondered whose it could be.

When I opened the door Molly looked serious and was holding a bouquet of flowers. It was too much. "My God, Molly! Tell me quickly. Who died?"

"It's Riki Ellsworth, an elder from Christchurch," she said. "Peta told me that he was special to you and didn't want to have you hear over the phone."

My God, my God! How could it be? My beautiful brown man in Christchurch whom I had never seen again but who had changed everything. I began to cry. More troubling, almost, than his death, was the strange timing of it. Not two weeks after the last of the pieces left New Zealand, this man who had feared so much for their safety, this man who had entrusted me with their care, was gone. What could it mean?

Douglas and everyone from AFA agreed that the new penis on the ridgepole from the Auckland Museum was an unfortunate addition. "Do you think they'll let us take it back off?" they asked. I had planned to phone Laurence Mann, the director of the Museum that owned the piece, to read him conservation treatment proposals, and agreed to find a diplomatic way to pose this question as well.

I did it in as humorous a way as possible, and we had a bit of a laugh over the phone. "I'll have to get back to you on all these issues," he said. "It's something I need to consult with the conservator about."

Several days later our publicist at AFA was working late. An overseas telegram came in by phone, and as she was the only one in the office, she agreed to take the message. The cable read: "All treatments approved except penis." "Excuse me," she said, "I believe I misunderstood you. Can you spell that last word for me please?" They spelled it back and forth four times, neither one willing to be the first to laugh.

The next morning I found the message on my desk with a note pinned to it: "What *is* this!!??" I planned to answer the cable but things were pretty frantic around the office. I'd checked with everyone at AFA and we agreed the penis was unfortunate but wasn't worth more time and effort to correct. With that decision made, I forgot all about it.

Three weeks later another telegram came in from Laurence Mann in Auckland. It read: "Please advise on penis refusal." By now I realized that Laurence was having a good time. I immediately sent off a cable that read: "We've decided to leave the penis alone." I pinned all three telegrams to my bulletin board.

When I next spoke to him, I found out he had done the same. "Thanks a lot, Laurence," I said. "I'm sure the international operators think I'm having a sex change operation!" I chuckled for weeks.

During the first week of August we began the installation of Te Maori at the Met. It went well but painfully slowly for various reasons, not the least of which was the union situation. "Let's do this one next," I'd say. "We have to wait for the packers to open the boxes," said the rigger. "Oh, but there's a box wrench right here," I'd answer naively. "The *packers* open the boxes," said the rigger through his teeth. "We need some padding for under this piece," I'd say. "I have some pads downstairs in the lab," said the conservator: "I'll go get them." "*I* get the padding," said the rigger. "*My* men take care of the padding." So we'd

wait and wait and wait. "Who are we waiting for now?" I'd say
brightly. "The box openers or the box closers or the pad get-
ters?" "We're waiting for the designer." "He just arrived. He's
right there." "Now we're waiting for the conservator. We're not
allowed to touch a piece unless a conservator is present." And
quietly, I'd count to ten, tell myself to remain calm.

The installation itself was torturous. I'd relaxed a little on
seeing that everything had made the trip in such good condition, but now was gripped by new anxieties. Every moment
seemed like the one when "it" was going to happen. I watched
the riggers preparing to hoist the massive figure of the chief
Pukaki and his two children high onto a pedestal. I watched as
the rigging straps stretched and creaked, straining to lift his
weight. Always, in the back of my mind, was Peta's voice . . .
"The only payment could be a life . . ."

In mid-August I took three days out from the installation at
the Met and flew to Chicago. There, I was to pack the silver
exhibition at the Art Institute and courier it to Miami. The trip
turned out to be one of those that can be viewed as a small
nightmare or a wild adventure, depending on one's frame of
mind. I wasn't exactly calling it a wild adventure, as I once
might have, but it had not yet reached the nightmare stage—the
point of no return. Conflicting feelings about my job, New York
and my life continued to battle one another.

Things were getting frantic now at the Metropolitan. Soon it
would be September 10, a day that had been worked towards for
nine years. At 6:32, the official time of dawn on that day, two
hundred invited guests would be gathered and waiting on the
steps of the Metropolitan Museum. We, the guests, would
include museum directors, scholars, officials from Mobil Oil,
foreign dignitaries, the press, AFA staff, the New Zealand
Consular staff and numbers of other people who would not often
again find themselves gathered in front of a museum at 6 A.M.
This odd event would repeat itself in St. Louis and again in San
Francisco as the exhibition proceeded on its tour. Always, no
matter what the hour, we would gather at the official time of

dawn and for each opening, a new group of elders and a different cultural group would be flown back from New Zealand to perform the sacred ceremony.

These arrangements had been made, in many ways, with greater difficulty than plans for the exhibition itself. Exhibitions we knew about. Dawn ceremonies we did not. There were hotels for the entire Maori contingent, protocol over whether the elders would agree to enter the museum the day before the ceremony for a dry run (they would not), concerns over the weather and how long the warriors, in loin cloths and bare feet, would be able to stand out on Fifth Avenue and of course, there had been concerns about cost. Over the years these issues had been resolved. The event that was about to take place would take place only because of the intricate web of support provided by Mobil, the National Endowment for the Arts, the National Endowment for the Humanities, Air New Zealand, the New Zealand Consulate, the AFA's National Patrons and the Metropolitan Museum itself. Anticipation and anxiety were great in these last days.

Soon the spirits of the Maori ancestors would officially begin their visit to America.

*   *   *   *   *

At first light I heard it. A pale dusting of morning crept between buildings in the east and with it came the greeting call. "Haere ma-a-i-i . . ." It rose above the city sounds, above the chortling of the early buses making their way down Fifth Avenue, off key, warbling a little, and then it reached a crescendo. The sound diminished softly into the hugeness of the city. Haere mai!— the quick, powerful response of the men. We stood along either side of the museum's main steps and watched in silence.

They moved slowly down the avenue from 84th Street as we strained our necks to see. In the lead was a tall, striking man with golden brown skin and a long mane of snowy white hair. The distance was still too great, but a little glimmer stirred in my memory. I struggled to see through the crowd. The procession moved slowly, chanting and praying, and the warriors danced ahead, thrusting with their spears, darting their eyes about, fending off the spirits, clearing the way for the elders of their land.

They reached the foot of the steps and turned to face us. Now I had a clear view. The tall man in the lead adjusted his feather cloak over his business suit. He took the first step and raised his head. It was Tommy! Tommy from the witch trials in Taranaki two years before. It was he who had sat beside me through that horrible day, he who had whispered in my ear to tell me what they wanted from me. It was he who had defended me.

The procession slowly passed us, disappearing into the Met. We followed. The elders moved through the museum, coming finally to the door, coming finally to the place where their ancestors stood proudly waiting. The chants and prayers grew louder as they made a full circuit of the hall, stopping for a moment in front of Uenuku, in front of Pukeroa and Pukaki, stopping here and there to lay green branches at their feet. The Americans, somehow, had become both hosts and guests in this house as we faced each other across the room.

The Maori speakers talked of pride and of love; ours of honor and joy. All spoke of hard work and vision. The speeches went on for some time and were interspersed by prayers and songs. When it was done, the room was still. People were asked to follow now to the formal breakfast. This they did with some awkwardness because the solemn mood was so hard to break.

I could stand it no longer, I broke away from the crowd, from the American side, and flew across the space in between. I ran up to the tall man with snowy white hair and with hands on my hips I demanded, "Are you Tommy! Don't you remember me?!" And then he looked. He threw his arms wide and I thought my ribs would break in his embrace as he uttered a cry and swept me off the floor.

At noon there was a formal luncheon at which many speeches of acknowledgment were made. There was a round of applause for

Douglas Newton, the guest curator of the exhibition, and murmurs of appreciation for others who had made this day possible. The final speech was given by Phillippe de Montebello, the Director of the Metropolitan Museum. He, too, acknowledged long lists of people for their contributions, and at the end he acknowledged the American Federation of Arts. "From AFA," he said, "I'd like to thank Wilder Green, Jane Tai and Jeanne Hedstrom." Then it was over. Everyone stood to leave. I would never have said this could matter to me, but in that moment, in that split second of silence where my name might have been, it mattered very deeply. Peta was across the room and at my side in seconds. "It's OK," he said, "you're in the Maori hearts. That's what counts."

I carried Peta's words with me all day. Later when Wilder Green, the director of AFA, apologized for the terrible oversight, I thanked him for the apology. But in the back of my mind I said Peta's words over and over and over, like a mantra, all day.

That evening, hundreds of people were gathered for the reception in the great hall of the Metropolitan Museum. Word spread through the crowd that New York's Mayor, Ed Koch, a special invited guest had arrived. Quickly, the Maori warriors abandoned their drinks and hors d'oeuvres, checked each other's tattoo-painted faces and gathered for the haka—the fierce and warlike dance that is used to greet important visitors. The crowd parted as a thunderous sound rose in the hall. The warriors stamped in unison and leapt forward, waving spears and shouting, slapping their chests in rhythmic patterns until their skin turned an angry red. The mob approached.

Mayor Koch's elated grin turned to a worried smile as they drew a bit closer than was comfortable. Spears flayed the air and his smile disappeared, his face becoming a bit taut and slightly pale as he bravely stood his ground, unwilling to offend by backing up. With a final, riotous shout, the warriors stopped, their spears and their faces only inches from the Mayor's. There was deafening silence. "I come in peace," said the Mayor in a small voice.

Two nights later some friends and I went out for Chinese food with Peta. Somewhere in the conversation I mentioned my first trip to New Zealand, how difficult it had been. "Yes," Peta said, "the word spreads fast in New Zealand. When you first arrived the word was about this American *girl* they had sent. But after a while," he continued, "you got to be 'Carol,' and by the time you left, the word was, 'Is she married? Maybe we can fix her up with someone.' "

"Peta!" I shrieked. "Why did you wait two years to tell me this!?" He answered, looking perplexed, "Because I thought you knew." Only then did I realize that I did know.

On Saturday evening the cultural group gave a performance in the auditorium of the American Museum of Natural History. There were nearly 1000 people packed into the hall and hundreds more were turned away at the door. By that time the dawn ceremony had appeared on the front page of the *New York Times* and in the centerfold of the *Daily News*. It had been on two morning network TV programs. A six-page story came out in *National Geographic, Time* magazine, *US News, The Village Voice, The New Yorker*—on and on the list went. New York had fallen in love with Te Maori.

The cultural group sang traditional Maori songs and danced and pantomimed the history of the Maori people in elegantly choreographed skits: their long migration from the islands of Hawaiki, the seven canoes led by Uenuku in the form of a rainbow; the years of being hunters and gatherers; the beginning of agriculture and a more stationary way of life that led to the development of carving and weaving skills. They talked of how in later years their people had been decimated and how their numbers had dwindled until the pride of those who remained had all but vanished. They spoke of drugs and alcoholism, unemployment and prison cells that held too many of their people. Then they spoke of a pride renewed. They spoke of Te Maori and how it had turned the world's eyes to them, how an appreciation of their art might bring with it a new appreciation of their people. "I am a Maori," the man said to a now silent room, and with this, the end of his narration, he called a few of us from the audience up onto the stage to join them in their final song.

They took our hands, we who were there to represent AFA, Mobil, the Consulate and the museums on the tour. They raised our hands high, clasped in theirs, and as they sang we all began to sway slowly back and forth with the melody. The song gained force and rhythm and through the glare of the television lights I was suddenly aware of movement in the audience. People began to stand. At first only a few, but then more and more until 1000 people were on their feet, 1000 people spontaneously linking hands, raising them above their heads. The song was louder now and the audience began to sway in rhythm with the people on the stage who swayed in rhythm with the whole room, which seemed to sway and dip and thrill to the sound of the voices blending and swelling. The leader of the cultural group moved to the front of the stage. Loudly, to be heard over the tremendous swell of voices, he called, "We want you to know . . . that you are now . . . all members . . . of the extended family . . . of the Maori people of New Zealand!" That is when the song ended, and when the audience went wild. Applause broke like thunder.

The opening events were over. Everyone flew home to New Zealand and on September 13 I flew to Tacoma, Washington to unpack and inspect the Mimbres pottery exhibition that was now midway through its tour of the United States. For nearly two years I had swayed back and forth between the urge to leave my job at AFA and the idea that it was AFA that provided the adventures in my life. In the moments when the job was most intense, when I was most frenzied and exhausted running from one city to another working on fifteen exhibitions at once, I knew it had been too many years and I must leave. In the calmer moments I glimpsed boredom and wondered what I could possibly do instead that would be as exciting and wonderful. Further complicating my already complicated feelings was the fact that leaving AFA also meant abandoning Te Maori midstream. It meant abandoning my silent promise to Riki Ellsworth, the beautiful brown man in Christchurch. Now, at some unidentifiable point during Te Maori's opening festivities, I knew I had reached a decision.

I could not leave my job. I could not leave because Riki had died and I could not leave because Tommy had hugged me. I could not leave because Peta had teased about marrying me off. It was not rational but I knew, finally, that whatever my personal needs, I could not abandon these people—either the living or the dead.

The decision was a relief. Now, instead of vagueness about my future there was a plan. I would continue at AFA and in January of 1986, would return Te Maori to its people in New Zealand. At that time I would finally be free to leave my job and New York and anything else I wanted to leave behind. It seemed like an eternity away from the vantage point of September of 1984; from the vantage point of one more Sheraton Hotel room in Tacoma. How many more adventures and how many more nightmares before January of 1986? But the decision was made.

When I got back from Tacoma, Wilder walked into my office. "Maybe you'd better sit down for this," he said. "How would you feel if the Maori show went on to Chicago?" "Do you mean *instead* of St. Louis or San Francisco?" I asked cautiously. "No, in *addition* to St. Louis and San Francisco," he said. "You mean it won't go home in January of 1986? You mean, like another booking on the tour so it doesn't go home until June of 1986? You mean that kind of thing?" "That's what I mean," he said.

I clutched my heart and slid into the chair. "I might die!" Then I started to laugh. It wasn't what he'd expected. He knew how I felt about the exhibition. Laughter wasn't what I would have expected either.

"Now, it still has to be explored," Wilder acknowledged, "but Field Museum of Natural History in Chicago is very anxious to have it." I said that certainly it was *possible,* and of course we'd have to watch carefully to see how the most fragile pieces fared in the next few months, to see if they could withstand the trip. I said there was also the matter of whether *I* could withstand the trip.

Fighting to keep the wild laughter down in my throat, I went on to say that we might have to budget for a conservator to review the pieces again before we made a decision, and I tried not to laugh while he went on to say that of course Field Museum had to be prepared to pay the fee for the exhibition as had the other museums on the tour, and that of course there would also be transportation costs and installation costs, "and," I interrupted, "funeral costs for your registrar." We laughed again.

It was the end of the day. I walked home from work, laughing my way up Park Avenue. How trustingly I'd hung my entire life around this exhibition. And what after Chicago? Then it might be, "How would you feel if the Maori show went to London?" I knew then what had to be done.

I took a few more weeks to digest the realization, and on November 14 gave notice at AFA, after seven years. March 29 would be my last day. I wondered if anyone would care. Would Peta care? Would Riki have cared? I decided they didn't care. In the next instant I wondered how it was, then, that *I* could still care so very deeply.

AFA sent out the word that they were looking for a new chief registrar. I offered to finish the tour of Te Maori on a freelance basis. AFA said that it sounded logical but cautioned against making assumptions. It had to be thought through very carefully from their point of view, they said. There were financial and logistical issues that had to be taken into account. This response distressed me. I had expected them to be pleased and relieved at my offer and had expected to leave the meeting feeling pleased and relieved myself. Instead I felt dull and blank, unable to think. I was exhausted and angry at the intensity of my own feelings for this strange exhibition which was, after all, just another exhibition.

On Sunday, January 6, I paid a final visit to Te Maori at the Metropolitan Museum, passing by, as I often did, after a morning run in Central Park. I wandered through, stopping in front of Uenuku and Pukeroa, stopping before Pukaki. I told them I would be by in the morning to start taking them down, that I would pack them up one more time and take them on to St. Louis. I told them it was still indefinite but I might be going away after that.

I listened very carefully. I stood in front of Uenuku and tried to tell if he cared. There were no answers hanging in the air that day, only sadness. I went home.

When the museum closed that night, the New York presentation of Te Maori ended. A little over 200,000 people had come to visit since September 10.

*   *   *   *   *

It was two degrees below zero fahrenheit on Monday morning, January 21. The worst had happened. On the day shipment number one was to leave for St. Louis, on the day five huge crates were to be carried back down the steps of the Metropolitan Museum, it was minus two degrees Fahrenheit. The steps were a sheet of ice. The wind was fierce. We aborted the plan.

I raced to AFA and pulled stacks of documents from the files. With lists of values, dimensions of crates and floor plans of the trucks I began to reshuffle the three shipments. Somehow, and quickly, I had to arrange things so that large crates needing to be carried down the steps did not have to go out the next morning.

That way, even if there was no break in the weather, one shipment of smaller crates could be loaded and on its way.

It had been 102 degrees when Te Maori arrived in New York—a rarity in a New York summer. Now that Te Maori was leaving it was minus two degrees—a rarity in a New York winter.

The truck was at the Met by 8:00 Tuesday morning and by 11:00 loaded with crates that could be brought down in the elevator. The driver was Joe McGinley whom I had not seen since a seventy-hour trip from San Diego to Detroit the previous winter when we'd almost frozen to death on the side of the road. He had a new partner, Mike Flannery. The courier on this truck was an art handler from the St. Louis Art Museum. Soon our first shipment was out the door.

It had been my plan always to have Uenuku with me—in this case, on the third shipment. But his crate was one of the smaller ones that didn't have to be carried down the steps. Because of the weather I had been forced to let him go without me, on the first shipment. A memory glimmered and began to drift elusively in the back of my mind. Then I had it. The Queen had said that if the exhibition was to go it must be led by the spirit of Uenuku.

Uenuku, at that moment, was leading the spirit of Te Maori to St. Louis. It was a bit extreme of him, I thought, to freeze the entire Eastern Seaboard just so he could go first. There were subtler ways he could have reminded me.

Joe called at 10:00 that night. He was in western Pennsylvania and had been forced to pull off the road. The weather was terrible. He said not to worry, that everything was fine. I said I trusted his judgment, just to be sure the reefer, the climate control unit, had plenty of fuel and that the truck, as always, was never left alone.

Joe called again at 4:30 A.M. His voice was different. "Hi, babe," but serious this time. No introduction. He knew I knew who it was. The reefer had jelled up. Stopped. It had only been down thirty minutes, but it was fifty degrees below zero out with the wind. The temperature in the trailer had fallen from 70 to 36 degrees in half an hour. I felt dull and blank. Uenuku was on board. The wood could split right down the middle from such a radical climate change. I felt angry again that we were risking so much. Joe said he had the truck inside at a truck stop—he had talked the mechanic into letting him take up the entire work bay. "He said I could keep it inside until he needs the bay," said Joe, "but I hid the keys. I won't pull it back out." "Pay him anything he wants, Joe, but don't pull out till the reefer is running," I told him. "OK, babe," he said. "We're working on it."

From then on my apartment sounded like the Jerry Lewis Telethon. The dispatcher called to say that Joe was back on the road, reefer running. I called St. Louis to tell them he had been delayed. The dispatcher called back to say that Joe would now never make it back to New York by Thursday morning to pick me up with the third shipment. Was Thursday afternoon OK? I called the Met. The Met called me back. I called St. Louis to say the third shipment would also be delayed. The dispatcher called back to say that Joe was now running into heavy snow and would be even later. I called St. Louis back. This went on and on. All day.

On Thursday the second and third shipments could be put off no longer. It was ten degrees out, which was probably the warmest we could hope for. Twenty-eight riggers gathered in the Sackler balcony at 7:00 A.M. They wheeled the crate with the Pukeroa Gateway slowly down long corridors until we stood, once again, at the top of the grand staircase. No one spoke. The riggers paused a few moments to collect their thoughts and their strength and on the count of three, they lifted. The way down was so much worse! The crate now had a momentum of its own that constantly had to be checked. The silence was painful, the struggle visible in the shuffling feet and straining backs.

Then came the voice of the head rigger . . . "Eight Maoris carried this crate in New Zealand," he said with a sneer. No response, only shuffling feet, pained breathing. His voice rose again, out of the silence . . . "Then they carried the crate out to the plane." Still no comment. The tension mounted as they neared the bottom. They were losing their grip. One more time his voice rose above the bent backs . . . "Then they carried the plane down the runway." Shoulders started to shake. A silent chuckle spread and then they were at the bottom. They slid the crate to the floor and a roar of laughter burst across the great hall.

We climbed the stairs to get the second of five crates. By noon, the second truck was loaded. Shipment number two was on the road with Cap Sease as courier.

I went home to have some lunch, gather my luggage and wait. At 2:00 one of the registrars from the Met called. "You're on!" she said. Joe and Mike had finally delivered shipment one and driven back through storms from St. Louis. They were rolling into the loading dock.

We didn't hit the blizzard until western Maryland. Joe, in the sleeper, was out like a light; Mike at the wheel. Within half an hour it was impossible to see ten feet. Walls of snow swirled up in front of the cab, swallowing the truck in white. We didn't even wait to find a truck stop or a place with facilities. "Grantville," the sign said. We took the turn-off. Snow was coming down in thick, horizontal slabs and the trailer swayed alarmingly with the ferocious winds. We crept into the deserted little town and pulled up for shelter close alongside the biggest building in sight—Historic Casselman's Restaurant. It was 10:00 P.M.

All night I watched the storm. Mike, in the bunk now, with Joe slumped across the driver's seat, slept on. Far down the road was a bank clock. "2:00," it flashed. "23 degrees." "2:32, 21 degrees." It disappeared in the whiteness for a while and then came back. "3:02, 19 degrees." I tried to think about how long it had been since we'd seen a bathroom. "4:15, 18 degrees."

At 5:00 I decided I was getting out in the storm to pee behind the truck. That's when the snow plough arrived. So much for a pee behind the truck. The plough's headlights cut in and out, jabbing the night, making tunnels of light in the falling snow.

At 6:00 the light went on in the house next door. At 6:15 a woman in a pink sweater dashed from the house through the storm and into Casselman's. At 6:30 I could sense that Joe was awake even though he had not stirred. "What do you want first," I asked, "the good news or the bad?" "Bad," came a voice from the motionless figure. "The storm is worse and the temperature is falling." "Shit. What's the good news?" "This restaurant is about to open."

That's when we moved. Simultaneously. Our doors flew open. We were on the ground, running around the front of the truck. We bumped into each other going up the steps, again going through the door. "Good morning, ma'am," Joe tipped his hat. "How are you ma'am? You wouldn't have a bathroom here, would you, ma'am?" She pointed. We thundered down the stairs, giggling like children.

Two hours later the storm paused to catch a breath and we made a break for it. At the end of the exit ramp, the one on which we'd pulled off the night before, were two abandoned tractor trailers. One was jackknifed, the other flopped over on its side.

In Kentucky it was black ice. "Hey, Joe?" said Mike as we drove down a long steep hill. "The trailer's comin' around." I looked in my side view mirror. Sure enough, the trailer had crossed the white dividing line. The tractor hadn't. The road looked deceptively like asphalt but was really covered with a thin sheet of ice. "Black ice," Mike said. The trailer had gone into a slide.

"Run away from it," said Joe, up on his elbows, leaning out of the bunk. By then we were already going too fast for a steep icy hill, but there was no other answer. Somehow, the tractor had to start going faster than the trailer to get back ahead of it. Mike ran the gas pedal slowly towards the floor. At first I thought it best not to speak, not to break his fierce concentration as he fought to stay in control. Then I thought it best that something be said. I said it quietly. "Mike, if you have to go, go your way, not mine." He jerked his head to me briefly, then back to the road. "I see what you mean," he said. On my side was a thirty-foot drop. On his, a stone wall.

At the bottom we laughed. "Why are we laughing?" I asked. "Because we're nervous wrecks," Mike said.

It got worse after dark. We'd passed thirty or forty cars alongside the road—flipped over, burrowed into the snow in the median strip, spun around the other way on the shoulder. There was one pile-up of seventeen cars and four tractor trailers. In Winchester we pulled into a Holiday Inn and parked the truck where we could see it out the window. Joe called the state police. "What are road conditions west of Winchester, Kentucky?" he said. "Let me put it to you this way," said the trooper. "You can drive if you want to, but there are so many accidents that the state police are no longer able to respond to accident calls." "That's it," Joe said. "We're shutting down."

I called the St. Louis registrar at her home. "Don't risk another mile!" she said. "We'll see you when we see you."

Joe walked up to the clerk at the Holiday Inn desk. Joe had his baseball cap on backwards. His hair was sticking out the hole in the front. He and Mike had a two-day growth of beard and I was wearing three ragged sweatshirts. My hair was matted and dirty. Joe swaggered a little bit, leaned an elbow on the counter and looked as cool and as tough as he could. "We need a couple 'a rooms," he said to the clerk. "And we need 'em where we can see our truck out the window. We're haulin' nuclear waste and if it starts to leak during the night we have to be able to see the cloud of smoke so we can evacuate the building."

The clerk's eyes never left us. His head tilted down to look at the reservation book but his eyes remained riveted on the apparition in front of him. Mike and I spun around, choked down our laughter and left Joe to his games. He had not warned us.

There were two inches of ice over the back doors of the truck.

Now, with the unexpected luxury of a room and a shower, we had no luggage. We would have to put the same clothes back on. I had a tube of toothpaste. Mike had a blow drier. That was all.

We used the adjoining doors to our rooms as a kind of mail drop. Joe knocked. "I'm putting the blow drier between the doors," he said. I waited to hear his door close. I opened mine and took the drier from the floor. "I'm putting the toothpaste between the doors," I said. He waited to hear my door close. I heard his open. "Send the drier back through when you're done," he said through the door. He and Mike took turns sleeping in the truck. They never called me for my shift.

It took us 48 hours in all for a trip that should have taken 23. It was horrible to see them drive away from the museum. The crates were safely inside. The trip was over. "What do you mean you're going off and I'm staying here!?" my mind screamed. "Shouldn't I be going with you?" It happens every time. We shook hands. They each gave me an awkward kiss on the cheek. "It was a fun trip," Joe said. Mike and I nodded and then it was time for them to leave. "Take care of yourself." It was hard for all of us. I could see it in their backs as they walked towards the truck.

We began unpacking the exhibition on Monday morning. "Can we open that crate first," I asked, turning suddenly in the sea of crates and pointing to box number four. "Anything you like," said John Nunley, the curator. "Why that one?" I didn't know and could see only that my attention had been drawn very strongly to box four. In it was the small stone figure belonging to the Queen. I had been careful to put it in my truck. The technicians unbolted the lid and set it aside.

"My God! What's this?" I said in alarm. The top half of the figure was covered with tufts of white. I scooped him out of the crate like a baby, blew on him, and the tufts floated away. They were bits of flannel. I must have put him in just slightly wrong when we packed the show in New York. His ear, riding a bit high, had been rubbing on the inside of the lid. It had worn through the flannel, depositing bits of fluff over the figure.

Only then did I remember something that had happened during the truck ride. Just before the blizzard I had noticed a pain in my stomach. The pain increased rapidly until I found myself rigid, gripping the edge of the seat, unable to speak. I wanted to tell Mike to pull over, that I was very sick, but the pain had taken my breath away. He looked over then, noticing that I was white as a sheet and sitting in a tortured position. We pulled off the road.

I was in a panic. Maybe I was having an appendicitis attack on a tractor trailer in the middle of nowhere. Mike looked upset. He could see I was very sick but could see also that soon the road would be impassable. The snow had begun. I waved him on. There was nothing to do. Eventually, after about an hour, the pain in my belly subsided as mysteriously as it had come.

Now I stood in the St. Louis Art Museum being stared at by a curator. In my arms I held the top half of a small stone figure that had been split across the belly centuries before and whose ear had been rubbing all the way from New York. His crate had been the first crate up on the right side of the trailer, just behind my seat.

I told John the story of my fierce bellyache in the truck. "I think he was just yelling to me," I said. " 'Hey! Get me out of here. My ear is rubbing!' " I made myself a note to adjust the crate so he would be more comfortable. John shook his head but the look on his face showed surprise rather than disbelief, delight rather than judgment. I was pleased by this.

Cap and I painstakingly and meticulously inspected the exhibition against the reports we had made in New Zealand in 1982. Cap had been brought back into the project to review the pieces and offer an opinion as to whether it was advisable to add the Chicago venue to the tour. Having both survived hair-raising trips from New York to St. Louis—her truck, having taken a slightly more northerly route, had also crawled through blizzards the whole way—we were both now opposed to the idea. The added venue would mean not only added wear and tear on very fragile objects, but also a trip through the northern Rocky Mountains the following January! It just didn't seem possible.

There was still no resolution as to whether I would be hired on an independent basis to complete the Te Maori tour for AFA. I became more and more convinced that no one on either side of the Pacific even knew I existed, let alone cared whether I continued to care for the exhibition. Until some decision was reached, however, I still considered it my responsibility to plan for Te Maori's future in America. I informed AFA that the pieces had all travelled well but that Cap and I both disapproved of the extension to Chicago.

We installed Uenuku first in St. Louis. Everyone agreed that this was the only way to begin. It was a simple process and within a short time he stood, elegant and powerful, alone in the corner of the gallery. We watched him for a few minutes silently, each absorbed by our own thoughts and impressions, and then we went to lunch.

There was a small green branch at his feet when I returned. "Where did this come from?" I asked the crew, feeling as if we had all slipped into the twilight zone. Had an invisible Maori elder crept into the gallery while we were gone? But no, Mary-Edgar Patton, the registrar, had been at the opening in New York. She had seen the elders place green offerings at Uenuku's feet. "I didn't think he should stand there with nothing," she said now. And we all nodded, because of course it was true.

That is how it started. "He's in that crate over there," I would say. Everyone laughed. But the next morning it was someone else. "Who are we installing first today?" they'd say. Again, everyone laughed. But soon they were calling them he and she and no one laughed, and soon they called them he and she and no one even noticed. Not very long after that there were strange looks if anyone referred to a piece as "it." Slowly, painstakingly, the show went up, one by one with scaffolds and hoists, tweezers and gentle care. As the rooms filled with solemn and powerful figures, they filled also with green branches. I no longer knew who brought them.

St. Louis, like Auckland, soon became home, and with this, the concept began to soften and shift under my feet. I was no longer sure just what home meant. My hotel room had a kitchen which I stocked with mongrel pots and pans from the five-and-dime. I found out where to buy the best produce and the freshest fish. Three meals a day in restaurants made me an outsider, but dashing home in the sleet with a grocery bag under my arm, I became a native. One Saturday I baked bread, surprising even myself by what can be done with a wooden spoon, a pot and two washcloths as pot holders.

In John Nunley I found a new running partner and, more than that, a good friend. We met often in Forest Park for a run in cold so bitter it can only be braved by two. Sometimes he would wander into the gallery a bit after we'd started work. "Good morning," he'd say, already focusing on the piece we were installing as he absently planted a kiss somewhere on the side of my head.

The crew at the museum scooped me up on Fridays to join them after work for a beer at Blueberry Hill, their favorite pub. There were occasional dinner parties and offers of sightseeing, and there were long, quiet hours alone with my journal or a good book.

In Te Maori I found an anchor, an exciting yet familiar friend. From St. Louis came friendship, and in the long hours of hotel room solitude came some pain and isolation, but finally peace and a quiet strength.

*   *   *   *   *

It was raining when the first grey light of dawn crept into the St. Louis sky just after 5:00. It was foggy but still the greeting call

rang clearly. Haere maaai . . . Haere mai! The elders began
from the foot of the steps, moving slowly in the lashing rain.
Morning followed them into the building and their voices
swooped and echoed and filled the huge entrance hall. Their
voices enveloped the people who waited inside the doors.

By evening, everyone was euphoric. By evening there had
been speeches and prayers, Maori songs, solemn moments,
laughter, food and a great deal to drink. At an informal party
after the evening reception the voices of the cultural group rose
in beautiful unison once more; not with a traditional Maori song
now, but with something else: "Meet me in St. Louey, Louey,
meet me at the fair . . ." Their voices filled the room with
laughter. An elder stepped forward to grab Jim Burke, the
Director of the museum, and the two men began to waltz.
"Meet me in St. Louey, Louey . . ." It went on and on until the
whole room was laughing, the whole room was dancing. It went
on until Jim Burke began to cry.

He broke away from the elder now and over the noise of the
joy that swirled through the room he spoke. He threw his arms
wide with laughter on his face and tears in his eyes and thanked
them all for the love and brotherhood that they had brought
from a land so far away. With a choke in his voice he said that
never, ever had he seen an event inspire such friendship and
good feeling among people and when the last word had barely
left his lips, he was whirled away again in another waltz, to
another chorus. "Meet me in St. Louey, Louey, meet me at the
fair . . ."

The morning after the opening there was a meeting in a confer-
ence room at our hotel. In attendance were the New Zealand
Minister of Internal Affairs, the Secretary of the Department of
Internal Affairs, the New Zealand Consul General from New
York, the Secretary of Maori Affairs, the Chairman of the New
Zealand Management Committee for Te Maori, the Executive
Officer of that committee, a New Zealand museum director as

spokesperson for the New Zealand museum community, the Director of Field Museum in Chicago, the curator of that museum, Douglas Newton from the Metropolitan Museum in New York and from AFA, Jane Tai, Wilder Green, Jeanne Hedstrom and me. The purpose of the meeting was to continue discussions on the advisability of sending Te Maori on to Chicago.

The meeting had been going on for hours, covering many aspects of the proposal, when Hekia Franklin stood up and said that as a spokesperson for the New Zealand museum community she now had to voice *their* concerns. She said that only one person in the world knew the entire collection and that person, she nodded down the table, was Carol. She said she had come to tell us that the museums of New Zealand would not agree to the extension of the tour unless they had absolute assurance of my continued association until the time of Te Maori's safe return to New Zealand.

Hekia went on. Speaking now as a Maori, she said, she was aware that I not only knew about the care of the objects but that I had developed a relationship with them. The Secretary of Internal Affairs then joined in and said that the continuity of care was essential to their granting permission for an extension of the tour.

Wilder did not even look down the table in my direction. Quickly he assured everyone that although I was soon to leave AFA, I would definitely be completing the Te Maori tour. We were asked to leave the room so that the New Zealand group could confer.

"Looks like you've got a job for the next year, doesn't it?" Jane said when we were outside the door. There was still funding to be secured, issues to be resolved, but if Te Maori was going to Chicago, so was I.

The opening was over. The meetings were done. We flew back to New York that afternoon.

*　　　*　　　*　　　*　　　*

March 1, 1985, New York

Lesley Abernethy
Auckland, N.Z.

Dear Lesley,

Only one month left at AFA! I can't really believe it, after nearly seven years. It's a bit harder to let go than I would have thought. I've been working for months on a really complicated project—arranging for an exhibition of ancient Eskimo ivories—and now I'm watching little bits of it being parcelled out to everyone else. One moment I want to volunteer to come in and finish the project, and the next, I know I won't care once I leave. Right now I'm sitting there watching someone else do my stuff. I forget that when I am not around to see all this, my mind will be on to other things.

The good news is AFA has not yet found a new registrar (it does my heart good. I would have been crushed if I'd been replaced within a week) and has therefore asked me to take on some freelance work for them after I leave. Perfect for both of us.

It was really hard to leave all those wonderful people at the St. Louis Art Museum. Will I ever get used to this? The solution, I suppose, is never to go anywhere, never to do anything intense and wonderful someplace else. Keep everything close to home and you won't be in a position to miss anyone or feel torn at leaving. Doesn't sound very exciting, does it?

It's starting to be spring here, thank God. The winter in St. Louis was ghastly.

Love,
Carol

April 1, 1985, New York

Lesley Abernethy
Auckland, N.Z.

Dear Lesley,

It's over. I am now self-employed, which at the moment could easily be confused with being unemployed. I will remain calm. There will be enough work. Yesterday was my last day at AFA and it was good that Jeanne had arranged a party at her house after work. That way we all swept out the door in a group and piled into cabs and it was good and confusing and distracting. Even so, it was hard. At the party I cried every time someone left to go home. I cried when a pink gorilla came to deliver a singing telegram and balloons. The gorilla was upset. It was a funny telegram and wasn't supposed to make me cry. The pink gorilla hugged me. Last night I wondered how I could be leaving something I've loved so much for so long. This morning I remembered. It's just time. I've never been clearer about anything.

Don't write or anything. I might die of shock.

Love,

Carol

On May 28, now operating on a freelance basis, I returned to St. Louis to take the show down again. John picked me up at the airport and drove right to the museum where we would begin work. It was wonderful to be back, to feel so familiar about the best place to park the car and what guard might be on duty at the south door. There were big smiles and hellos from everyone. "Welcome back!" they all said, "We missed you."

The Forest Park Hotel had given me the same room so I would feel at home and had even saved my pots and pans. The maid brought them upstairs, carefully wrapped in plastic. John and I met for a run in the park that very first day, picking up on conversations left dangling months before. We ran now, battling the sultry summer heat of St. Louis, as we had earlier fought its bitter winter cold. Again there were Fridays at Blueberry Hill for a beer with the crew and one Saturday, a twenty-mile bike ride with John and the mount-maker from the museum. We cruised the rolling Missouri farmlands, passing Daniel Boone's home, walked up some of the hills and stopped in the town of Augusta for the best French toast we'd ever eaten. I had not been on a bike in at least a year and the next day called John to say I was feeling the ride. The only comfortable thing to sit on, I reported, was the toilet seat. Aside from that I was doing a lot of standing up.

At work we functioned smoothly and evenly as before, a wonderful team. We were proud of one another, delighted with one another. The days were filled with good humor and hard, hard work as we tucked Te Maori back into its crates.

In the middle of the second week my former assistant from AFA flew in from New York to courier the first shipment to San Francisco. Uenuku was going first, no argument. On the morning the truck was to arrive I found a small plastic bag with three red carnations on Uenuku's crate. "What's this?" I asked, looking around at everyone. "I grew them from seed," said the man who was head of the installation crew. "I didn't think he should go off with nothing."

By noon the truck was loaded. Uenuku and his red carnations were on their way. We packed what remained of the exhibition in the rest of that week and on Monday the second shipment went out with a registrar from the deYoung Museum in San Francisco as a courier.

The mood was subdued now at the St. Louis Museum. The galleries where Te Maori had stood were empty and instead of echoing with laughter and voices and song, they echoed with silence. Already the painters had moved in to prepare for the next installation.

On Tuesday night at the hotel I packed my things. I finished the last of the food in the refrigerator and emptied the closets, stacked the pots and pans for the maid to take home if she wanted, and tried to read but couldn't. I tried to write in my journal but could not deal with the sadness that flowed onto the pages. I sprawled dumbly, blankly in the armchair, quietly humming, "Meet me in St. Louey, Louey, meet me at the fair . . ." The tune went over and over, absently, in my head. Quietly I prepared myself for morning. In the morning I would leave.

The phone rang then, jolted me out of the chair and out of my stupor. "It's Joe," he said. "Mike and I are in a truck stop 70 miles out of St. Louis and we're coming to take you to dinner." I flew into the bathroom, washed my face, pulled a clean shirt back out of the suitcase, ran down to the desk to find out if they could suggest "where it might be possible to park a 45-foot tractor trailer overnight." I booked a room for Joe and Mike and ran upstairs to finish the packing I'd been putting off till later.

When the truck arrived I could hear it a block away. My room was in the back of the hotel but that particular rumble, that particular sound I could have picked out anywhere. By the time I got downstairs Joe had talked the manager into letting him keep the truck right in front of the hotel. It took up most of the block. We walked around the corner to a restaurant on Euclid and sat outdoors at wooden tables. We talked and talked and laughed and laughed about everything that had happened to each of us since they'd dropped me in St. Louis six months before.

I reminded them of my bellyache on the truck and told them about the Queen's stone figure with his rubbing ear. They were stunned, they loved it. I told them how that very piece had turned out the lights in Waikato and then lost the film. "We wouldn't happen to have this guy on our truck again tomorrow, would we?" said Joe. "He's *always* with me," I said. "Oh, brother," Joe said. "Oh, boy. We're in for it now. Blizzards in June. I can see it all now. We'd better be real nice to these Moo-ees, Mikey," he said. "There aren't going to be any blizzards in June," I said. "And Joe—if you don't stop calling them Moo-ees . . . you're going to be struck by lightning."

That night the rains came. Tornadoes had been ripping through the midwest for two weeks. St. Louis was under a tornado watch but the weather had held. Shipment number one went off under only threatening skies and shipment two in a light grey drizzle. Now the storms had come to St. Louis. All night the thunder crashed, hurling me out of my bed to close the windows, out to open them again when it got too hot and sultry, out to close them again when I woke in a flash of lightening to find the curtains standing out straight, to find the wind roaring through the room. I imagined I heard every Maori ancestor in every crevice of the universe, protesting one more uprooting. In my troubled sleep I knew how they felt.

In the morning the sky boiled black and grey and brown but there was no rain. "Maybe we can make it," Mike said. "Maybe we can get loaded and on the road before it opens up again."

We drove slowly through Forest Park to the museum, through the bending, lashing trees. It began to drizzle as the first crate went out the door. We draped huge sheets of plastic over each crate now to protect them for the few yards from the museum to the truck. By the third crate the wind was up, whipping the sheet of plastic in our faces, tearing at our clothes. Then it was time for Pukeroa, the biggest and last crate. Suddenly the sky opened and the rain came down in sheets. It came from every direction at once until the trees seemed about to rip apart from their tortured gyrations.

"Plastic?" said Joe. "No plastic," I said. "It will blind us. We will lose our grip. We're about to see how waterproof these crates really are." The crate was out the door, its huge flat surface flooded in seconds.

We were drenched now, our shirts glued to our backs. The crew struggled with the crate and fought with the wind, our hair plastered to our heads. The crate was up on dollies. We wheeled it towards the truck, pushing one end into the door and trying to position it, fighting to make it go gently over the lip. "Run it in, now!" yelled Joe, shaking his head. "We just have to run it in now. It's getting soaked!" We saw that he was right. I nodded and everyone pushed and heaved, knowing that the water could do far worse than the bumps. And then it was in.

Fifteen soaking wet people grabbed huge cotton sheets from the back of the truck and swarmed around the crate, mopped at it, soaking up the water as well as they could.

I went to say goodbye. They stood now, just under the over-

hang of the door: John and Barbara, Tony, Mary-Edgar, Jonathan, Rick, Arthur, Bill and Mike. I stood in the pouring rain
because it no longer mattered, because I was already too wet to
care. I flapped my arms at my sides and shook my head at them.
"I'm going to miss you," I said. They nodded and forced their
faces to smile. I started to hug them, one by one, and Joe's voice
came through the storm, calling my name. I turned to look and
the truck was buttoned up now, equipment on board, doors
padlocked. He gave a thumbs up sign.

   "Let's pull it out of here," he shouted, and there was no more
time. I looked back at their faces. "Guess I have to go now," I
said, and we all just nodded, and then I was gone. Jonathan
walked alongside the truck all the way out, guiding us through
the narrow driveway. The last of Te Maori was on its way to San
Francisco.

                    *   *   *   *   *

Twenty minutes out of St. Louis I smelled wires burning. "No,"
Joe said, "it isn't us . . ." and then, "maybe it is," and we pulled
off the road. He opened the dashboard and found that two wires
had shorted out, burned through the plastic housing. "That's
our trailer lights," said Mike. "We've got no running lights." So
Joe turned off the lights which had been on because the sky was
so darkened by the storm.

   The first truck stop had a three-hour wait for repair service.
The next was fifty miles away and when we arrived, had a two-
hour wait. Joe got out and looked around under the back of the
trailer. "We could probably fix it," he said, "but it will take
hours to trace those lines." We drove on silently, worried
because cars were beginning to turn on their lights. Dusk had
replaced the darkness of the storm we'd left behind.

   "I'm going to turn the lights on," Joe said. "They won't burn
up in just half an hour or so and we have to get at least to the next
truck stop." He turned them on and I could sense that we were
all on edge. Soon, though, we looked at each other and the

edginess eased. There was no smell of burning wires. It was by now completely dark.

"What do you think?" I asked, and Joe said it seemed to be OK now, why didn't we just see how far we could get since we'd already lost so much time. Soon we forgot all about it. The night wore on forever and my head nodded endlessly against the door until a soft light began to creep into the sky, until in the side view mirror I saw a fiery orange ball pop over the horizon and insert itself into the morning.

"My God, Joe! Look at the beautiful sun just behind us!" and then, "and I smell wires burning again!" "You're right," he said, "and it's worse than yesterday." A thin line of grey smoke crawled out of the dashboard. "But listen," Joe said, staring into his side view mirror, "the sun just came up." There was silence as we thought about this. "The sun just came up, so I'll turn off the lights now!" We smiled at each other, realizing what had just happened. "Right," I said, "there's plenty of time to get them fixed before dark." But Joe said, "No, the Moo-ees are going to fix them." We both laughed but I looked at him strangely because he had said this with more conviction than I thought appropriate. "That's very cute, Joe, but we're getting the lights fixed by tonight." And again he said, "No, the lights will be fine by tonight."

So all day I fought with this in my head; all day I told myself not to be a nag and that it was his truck and he knew what he was doing. All day I asked myself why we wanted to wait until dark to start fussing under the truck to fix the lights.

Then it was dusk. Cars' lights began to flare on and Joe, too, reached out and flipped on the lights. I waited smugly. Soon there would be smoke. I stared at the dashboard and waited. We drove another few miles and there was no smoke. Now I began to laugh and Joe and Mike began to laugh. "I think the Moo-ees like us, Mikey," said Joe. We stared at the dashboard until I yelled, "Where is the goddamned smoke!?" We drove all night. At dawn, a thin curl of grey smoke made its way out of the dashboard. Joe turned off the lights for the day.

Our wet clothes from St. Louis had dried on us like cardboard but it didn't seem to matter. There were long quiet hours and lots of talk, lots of laughter and spectacular country to watch and admire as it flew by the windows. Whenever we stopped, Joe said he was going back to check on the Moo-ees, and this I found wonderful. I had never before seen him open up the truck on a long haul and check the shipment so frequently.

As always, Joe and Mike teased the hell out of each other and slowly, in the joy of this trip, my thoughts turned away from those left behind. I began to think of all the friends I had in San Francisco and all the new ones I would make. Slowly my thoughts turned to all that was about to happen rather than all that had gone before.

In Colorado we stopped for breakfast. Always there were strange looks in truck stops because three people in a tractor trailer is one too many, especially when one of them is me. I was used to the looks. We were getting one now from the waitress, even as she pretended to be looking down at her order pad. Joe leaned back in his chair, silently scanning the menu. With no change in expression he nodded towards me, "My wife here will have the pancakes." There was silence. "And our son," he said nodding towards Mike, "wants the fried eggs." Mike and I held it together this time. Our faces remained blank, impassive, as we looked up at her. The waitress, apparently unable to cope, simply walked away.

"I've never felt so dirty in my life," I moaned to Mike on the second day. "If we don't get to a shower soon I'm going to need a paint scraper to get these socks off my feet." "Are you kidding?" Mike said. "I'm gonna need an acetylene torch to get my underwear off!"

The truck seemed to travel at a ferocious speed but the miles to slip behind slowly. A private language of the road soon developed. "You know," Mike would say, "I'm not even slightly hungry." "No," I'd answer, "and I don't have to go to the bathroom either." Later Joe might say, "I don't need a shower at all," to which Mike would respond, "Neither do I, and I'm feeling really rested. I could drive another six hours."

After one long shift in the bunk Mike rolled up the vinyl curtain to see where we were and what time of day it was. He poked his head out, bleary-eyed and incredibly dishevelled. He looked at me with a serious, blank face and said quickly, "Is my hair perfect? Don't lie to me, now, I have to know. Is every hair in place?"

The truck pulled its weight more slowly as we entered the pine forests, the foothills that would take us into the Sierra Nevada mountains. At the top, hours later, in the Donner Pass, we stopped for a moment. We watched a hawk hang motionless over the lake, eyes searching for prey, and then we drove on. The Donner Pass was beautiful but also frightening, even in June. "Six percent downgrade next three miles," the sign said. "Suggest 45 mph." "Carry min. power," said the next; "Let 'er drift. Let 'em cool." "Three percent downgrade next five miles. Suggest 6-10 lb. brakes." Each sign was big and yellow and started with "Truckers!" in bold black letters. The signs talked them down the hills in trucker lingo. Too many had burned out their brakes on this mountain. Too many had, with mounting and uncontrollable speed, aimed for the runaway truck ramps and missed. I thought about January. In January we would come back through these mountains en route to Chicago. Then there would be snow and ice.

At the deYoung Museum in San Francisco we took the crates off the truck and wheeled them, one by one, down to the exhibition gallery where those from the first two shipments already waited. I looked around the room, my eyes searching for Uenuku. Someone had removed the carnations and put, in their place on the crate, a bunch of fresh yellow roses.

The registrar who had couriered the second shipment came out to the loading dock and we traded notes about the trip. "Oh," I said, "we had a bit of trouble with the lights just out of St. Louis, but otherwise things went fine." "That's funny," she said. "We lost our trailer lights right outside of St. Louis too but they just seemed to fix themselves." She took me to my hotel. I had by then been up for 56 hours, and in the morning we would begin, once again, to unpack Te Maori.

This is how it began in San Francisco. "What's with the flowers on the crate?" someone said. "There were some wilted carnations we thought might be important so we replaced them." I explained how the elders had left offerings in New York and how the staff in St. Louis had continued the custom. As we unpacked and inspected, while still in their crates and after they were installed, Uenuku and others never went a day without fresh greens. Sometimes the guards brought them, sometimes the crew or the conservators.

Weeks went by and as we worked I told them stories. I told them about the lights in Waikato and about the bellyache. I told them about the lights in the tractor trailer. The work was hard for me now. It was the seventh time I had inspected the pieces, the third time I had installed them. The work was slow and sometimes tedious but it was the people who changed it; it was the faces of the people as they gathered around. "We need only four to lift this piece," I would say, but everyone came over anyway. They shook their heads in wonder, smiled with pleasure. "God! He's a beauty, isn't he? I think that's my favorite," and then, "No! This is my favorite." Slowly, over the days, the crates emptied and the rooms filled.

During the installation, two terrible things happened. A plexiglass vitrine was being lifted onto a pedestal and slipped, making a nick in the eyebrow of a small head carved from pumice. The damage was very minor but to me, it was a warning. I had promised to take care of them and had let this happen. It seemed to me that I had become too casual, had allowed the joy that each new group of people took in this task to become too much fun. Perhaps I had become too tired. I gritted my teeth and wrote to the lending museum in New Zealand, explaining the incident and asking permission to restore the damage.

The second terrible thing was also a damage. We spent an entire morning installing the front of a carved meeting house. It took large numbers of people, equipment and elaborate choreography. When it was done we stood back to admire our work. I gasped. Steve and Elizabeth, the conservators, also gasped. The foam padding had peeled back. The metal brackets that held the piece on the wall were now gouging into the wood. Though they were tiny marks, I could not remember anything this horrible ever happening to a work of art in my care— something like this that could easily have been prevented. I should have checked the brackets. I should have been more thorough in my planning of every step of the installation. I felt that the moment I had dreaded was upon us. Luck was beginning to run out. The show's extension to Chicago, an idea I had gradually grown accustomed to, now seemed more frightening than ever before.

Steve and I discussed what to do. We decided that what damage had been done had been done. It would get no worse and so it was better to wait until the show came down in January and deal with it then. The gouges were very small; the pain they caused, extreme.

Nothing changed visibly after these two incidents. Everyone was a bit subdued for a few days and we all felt terrible, knowing that in some way we had each contributed to the injuries. Mostly what changed was my attitude. I felt I had been reminded, and I took the warning seriously. The days of work returned to normal with only the slightest shift in perception.

San Francisco was as much of a thrill as always. I stayed, this time in a Victorian bed and breakfast inn on Stanyan Street, the eastern edge of Golden Gate Park. There were old friends, lovely new ones at the museum, hikes in the Marin Headlands, Golden Gate Park with its flower gardens, waterfalls and lakes and as often as possible, there was the ocean. It was too cold to swim, but there I would sit for hours. Sometimes in late afternoon I watched the sun sink over the freighters that seemed never to move on the horizon. I listened to the waves lap, looking to the west and to the south. I pierced the distance with my eyes, trying to see, with clear dream vision, two islands floating in a distant sea.

*   *   *   *   *

We could not yet see the elders when the greeting call came in San Francisco. It came from behind the trees of Golden Gate Park, from the direction of the Japanese Tea Garden. An eerie, wailing voice rose with the dawn . . . Haere maa-iii . . . and faded into the rose bushes. They moved more slowly this time, hardly seeming to move at all. The procession made its way past the lily pond, up the ramp and into the deYoung Museum. Haere mai! We followed.

We listened in silence to the speeches. In the glare of the television lights, the explosion of flash bulbs, we watched as one after the other, speakers stood. The Americans said how honored we were, how Te Maori had touched and captured America. They told how grateful we were at having been entrusted with the care of these sacred and beautiful treasures and how seriously we took that honor and that trust.

The next man who stood did not look up. He was the last Maori speaker, and as he rose from his chair he shuffled a bit with his hands in his pockets. We watched. When he did look up he was shaking his head and said, "No." He shook his head again, pausing, searching, it seemed, for a word or a feeling. He looked up at the expectant faces now. "No," he said again, "*you* honor *us.* You have given us a larger place to stand in the world." His hands were not in his pockets now but were spread wide, embracing the room, the people, taking in the gaze of Uenuku who watched from a slight distance. The man went on in a room now silent as stone.

"We know," he said, "that our children and our children's children can come here to this marae, to your house *forever,* and that your children can come home to ours." It was time then for the president of the museum's board of trustees to speak. He rose from his chair in a silence so deep that time was suspended.

All morning, quiet and mysterious emotion had been building. Slowly, a liquid of feeling had been rising in those who watched, in those who listened. It was the same liquid that had filled us on another morning in St. Louis and as before we were puzzled by it. It was hard to know in just what way these simple words and simple ceremonies, in what way these people touched us as they did. The president of the board stood and opened his mouth to speak. He began to cry instead.

The words caught, choking, in his throat, and he brushed at his eyes. "Excuse me," he said shakily, "I seem to be having a bit of trouble with my composure." Many were crying now. Shoulders shook, heads bowed as people fought to control the emotions that welled from long hidden places. I no longer fought, but left my face to contort, the tears to flow into the collar of my blouse. The room was electric. The people of San Francisco too now belonged to Te Maori as much as Te Maori belonged to them.

November 29, 1985, New York

Lesley Abernethy
Auckland, N.Z.

Dear Lesley,

Well, it's finally dawning on me what the problem is here. Te Maori, and New Zealand, in fact, have spoiled me. I've been on the road for several weeks slogging away over two other shows. I tried to figure out why I was doing this and for some reason kept thinking of when I was out at Brian's farm for the shearing of his flock. They had missed eight sheep in the muster and there we were, just three of us running like mad things through the hills, trying to find eight sheep on 240 acres. I was beginning to think it was nuts, that we should just let the eight go and they'd get shorn next time around but Brian must have heard me thinking. "These sheep are bred as wool producers," he said.

"Their wool has become so thick now that if it rains they will be too heavy. They won't be able to get up and they'll die." We had, I realized then, passed several mouldering, rotting heaps in the hills that morning, mouldering heaps that used to be sheep before they got missed in the last muster.

It was the very first time in my life that I can recall a one-to-one correspondence between what I was doing and why I was doing it.

I went to a lecture at Columbia University a while ago. Some curator, just a normal, youngish guy in a dapper suit, put a slide of one Egyptian heiroglyph on the screen and obsessed about it for two hours! When he was done he triumphantly declared, "And so, I have now proven that the middle period of Egyptian history was 250 years longer than is believed by the leading German . . ."

There is room for this in the world too, you know? It's important stuff. But all I could think about while he was talking were the mouldering heaps of wool that used to be sheep. It scares me that I might have gone my whole life with all of the one experience and none of the other. It creates a really skewed perspective, I think, about the world and what's important.

And how does Te Maori fit into this? Well, with Te Maori, when I'm exhausted and ask myself why I'm doing this, the answer is that I'm working hard to protect and care for somebody's ancestors. The answer is that I'm doing this so a New Zealand Maori can stand in front of a crowd in a New York auditorium and say that his people, who have been downtrodden, have gained new pride. I'm doing this also so that the director of a sophisticated museum can cry and waltz around the room with a Maori elder. If it's not about people, I don't want to do it any more.

True, I might starve to death if I decide to adhere to this principle, but the feeling grows stronger and stronger.

I'll call you on Christmas morning . . .

Love,
Carol

I returned to San Francisco on January 5. In the months in between it had become definite that we were going to Chicago. When I arrived at the deYoung, Lesley and Elizabeth, the conservators, told me why it had taken so long to send us photos of the pumice head that New Zealand had given us permission to restore. Steve had touched up the damage and taken pictures of the repair. When he developed the roll of film there was nothing on it, so he assumed, of course, that he'd been in a hurry and that the film hadn't engaged. He took more photos and then lent the camera to the decorative arts curator in the museum. When that roll was developed the curator's photos had turned out but the ones of the Maori head had not—even though they were on the same roll of film. The conservators all went up to the gallery and tried once again to photograph it but the camera's light meter wouldn't work. They took it to be repaired. When they picked it up the man in the shop said there was nothing wrong with the light meter and the batteries were fine. "I can't help you," he said. They took the camera back to the gallery and tried again. The light meter still wouldn't work. They began to be suspicious then and Elizabeth had an idea. She took the camera elsewhere in the museum and photographed some Chinese porcelains. The light meter worked fine. They went back once more to the Maori galleries and began to talk to the pumice head.

"In no way do we want to hurt you any further," said Elizabeth. "We know you've been frightened, but it's necessary to take a few pictures to send back to your people in New Zealand so they can see that you're all right. After that we'll leave you alone and you can rest quietly again." The light meter worked. Elizabeth took the pictures and they came out fine. We sent them to New Zealand.

Later, one of the handlers who had been putting the vitrine on when it slipped, asked me how upset the lending museum had been about the damage. They agreed that it was unfortunate but minor, I told him, and he responded with surprising force, "Well, I don't think the *piece* felt that way about it!"

It was time to deal with the house front that had been gouged during the installation. The sight of the gouges, which I'd put out of my mind over the last months, was as distressing as ever. As soon as the panels of the house front were down the crew asked what I thought. "We can't tell anything until I get these mounting brackets off and turn the pieces over," I said. Once the panels were face up on pads on the floor I began to look for the gouges. I couldn't find them, and brought over a rolling inspection lamp since it was a bit dark at that end of the room. I still couldn't find them. I called Lesley and Elizabeth over to help and the three of us together couldn't find any gouges. "This is crazy," I said. "We're obviously looking in the wrong place." I reassembled the brackets and placed them on top of the piece, noting where the hooks would have fallen. There were no gouges. There were no scratches. There was nothing to indicate that anything had been wrong.

That night I was on the phone with Jeanne Hedstrom at AFA in New York. "You mean they mended themselves?" she screamed when I told her. "Well, something like that," I said. "Sort of like a self-cleaning oven." I explained just how the story had unfolded. When I got to the part about how we'd decided that the damage would not get worse over the next months, Jeanne interrupted. "*Au contraire!*" she said.

It took nearly two weeks to do condition reports on the entire exhibition. Of all the operations required to properly care for Te Maori, this one was tedious and the one that took real effort for me to get through. By the second week, with only a handful of pieces still to inspect, I had to force myself to maintain the rigid attention necessary to see that a crack had not grown a milimeter wider, a splinter was no weaker than it had been—by that time I always had to coax myself to remain alert. "Just a little bit more," I'd tell myself. "Just get through these last few and it will be three whole weeks before you have to do this all over again in Chicago."

On Wednesday of the last week, with great relief, I finished inspecting the last of the 174 objects. My mind raised an imaginary glass of champagne and I was about to make a big flourish of the fact that I was signing off on the last piece. I looked around the gallery to find everyone else working quietly at some task. I felt suddenly that it would be a silly thing to do. "Just sign the book and be done with it," said a voice in my head. I wrote the catalogue number of the piece I'd just inspected, #92, then the date 1/15 and signed my name next to it. As I turned away from the table all the lights went out in the gallery. A technician looked up and put his hands on his hips. "OK," he said. "which one turned out the lights this time!?" "Right here," I said, pointing to #92. "He's the last one to be inspected."

Later that afternoon, realizing there was a long holiday weekend ahead, I made flight reservations to go to Seattle for a visit. "Your return flight number will be 92," said the travel agent. I held the phone under my chin, watching my hand and the pen and the number 92 on the page. I felt vaguely distracted by something about it. "It departs Seattle at 1:15," the travel agent went on.

I wrote 1:15 next to the 92 and now saw why it disturbed me. I had just written this only a few hours before. Catalogue #92 on 1/15—the piece I'd been inspecting when the lights went out. I wondered what, if anything, it could mean and then began to laugh. Suddenly, in my mind was a cartoon image. All 174 of the Maori pieces stood in the gallery with their hands on their hips. "What do you mean you're going off to Seattle and leaving us here!?" they said. They stamped their feet. "You get back here right away!" I felt like someone's mother—or perhaps like someone's child.

When flight 92 dropped me back in San Francisco I checked into my hotel and walked through the park to the museum. I knew that it would already be closed but I went anyway. I did not need to go inside. I stood for a few minutes where I could see the building through the trees. I stood until something inside had been satisfied and then turned and walked back to the hotel.

The next day I went to Ocean Beach. It would be my last

visit. This time I stood in the water watching my feet turn red from the cold. The waves lapped at my ankles and swirled away. I stared at this water until I saw, in the late afternoon sun, tiny particles of light twirling and playing in rings around my toes. The rings of light grew larger and spread away in front of me until finally I looked up. The sun dazzled and jumped at the tips of the waves and I looked to the west and to the south. Faintly in the distance I saw beautiful brown faces waiting patiently and with some concern. I told them we were making a detour, going back into the country for a little while, and then we would be coming home. I said we were all fine and it was only a matter of a few more months. I sent these thoughts, in the swirls and eddies of light, to the west and to the south and then I walked back to the car where my friend Rudy waited.

"What were you doing?" he asked. "Putting a message in a bottle," I said. He nodded.

Pamela Forbes, the editor of the deYoung Museum's magazine, told me a story. After the opening in July, when I'd already left San Francisco, the Maori group was sightseeing in Berkeley. There they somehow encountered a group of American Indians, Zuni from the Southwest, she believed, and invited them to attend the final ceremony at the museum. It was after this ceremony that the Maoris were to return to New Zealand.

Pamela said that several Maori elders had spoken first at the ceremony. Then, as is the Maori custom, they invited the Zunis, their guests but also their hosts in this land, to speak as well. One of the Indians stood. He spoke for a long time in Zuni, his own language, and then he paused and looked at the brown faces in front of him. He must have found them familiar yet strange, and the eyes that looked back only a mirror of his own. Softly, and with deep emotion, he said, "We have waited a long time for you to come."

Pamela's eyes reddened and brimmed over. She shook her head, unable to continue, and I smiled at her in silent agreement, blinking away my own tears. We sat for a few moments while I puzzled at a wave of feeling so huge, so powerful that it threatened to burst from my chest, and then we went back to work. The line repeated in my head all day . . . "We have waited a long time for you to come."

Because of the terrible winter trip to St. Louis the previous year, I'd consulted with Cap about what else we could do to protect the pieces even further against climate changes during the upcoming trip to Chicago. I wanted to do something that would buy us a few more hours in the event that the reefer went out again. She suggested that we put lots of cotton flannel in the crates. The lids should be left off for a few days while the crates were still at the deYoung, giving the flannel time to absorb the ideal atmosphere of those galleries. Then, once the crates were sealed, the flannel would help hold the right humidity inside for quite some time. I ordered several bolts of white cotton flannel and as we packed each piece we first draped him in the soft, fuzzy cloth. At one point I heard somebody call out, "Don't close that crate! He doesn't have his jammies on yet." Only after each was wearing his fuzzy white pajamas were the lids bolted on.

Cap had just been hired as the new conservator at Field Museum in Chicago. This seemed right. She had been the first conservator to inspect the objects in New Zealand in 1982 and would now, bringing things full circle, be the last to inspect them before they went home.

On Monday, January 13, the first shipment left for Chicago with an art handler from the deYoung as courier. I waited, never far from a phone, for two days. He called on Wednesday. They'd made the trip in less than 48 hours. There had not been one flake of snow even in the Donner Pass. There weren't even any wet roads. Cap flew in from New York to courier the second shipment. She too called in less than 48 hours. Not a flake of snow and dry roads all the way across. It was incredible, really. We were crossing the Sierra Nevadas, the Rocky Mountains; we were crossing Wyoming and Nebraska and the midwest, and we were doing this in late January. No snow? No wet roads?

After yet another wrenching goodbye, I waved to a long line of smiling sad faces on the loading dock and got on the third truck bringing up the rear on Wednesday, January 22. We never saw any snow either and we never saw any wet or icy roads. As we passed through each state though, we'd hear on the radio that a storm center was heading for the place we had just left five hours earlier. We cruised through Utah and a storm hit Salt Lake that night. We zipped past Cheyenne and the Wyoming radio stations called for snow. We zoomed across Nebraska and on reaching Omaha, its eastern border, heard that storm warnings were in effect. We arrived in Chicago in under 48 hours. It took a long time to get all the crates off the truck and into the museum, and as the last crate passed through the doors and into the building, it began to snow.

The rest of the winter, the news reported, was a disaster. Nine feet of snow in the Rockies. Mud slides in California. Torrential rains and blizzards sweeping across the plains states, burying farms and highways. Chicago itself had a relatively mild winter. This seemed a bit odd.

While the crates were coming off the truck in Chicago, several people asked about the green branches. I explained, and mostly people just nodded their heads or smiled and said, my, wasn't that interesting. Two weeks went by while Cap and I unpacked and inspected. The now-dried branches from San Francisco remained next to many of the pieces. No one brought new ones. It disappointed me, but it seemed to be something that either had to happen on its own or not at all. The people were lovely and friendly and professional, but it was sad to think that the wonderful spirit that had followed Te Maori around the country had come to an end.

During the first days at Field Museum I ran back and forth between the condition reports and the preparators, showing them how the mount for each piece was to be attached to the walls. Odd things began to go wrong. Silly things that we shrugged off, but scratched our heads over, too. "We're smarter than this," said the head preparator, as we stood looking at one of the mounts that had been adjusted because of their lower ceilings. One of its legs had been cut shorter than the other. They were small incidents but there were many, and to me it seemed that a general feeling of resistance hung in the air. I began to come in early in the morning, before the crew arrived.

On the third morning, walking around the silent exhibition hall, I knew what was wrong. San Francisco was to have been the last stop on the tour. The next time the lids came off the crates, Te Maori should have been home in New Zealand. So we sailed through the mountains and across the country without a hint of the troubles of previous moves. But now, voices hung all around me in the silent room. "Chicago?! What the hell are we doing in Chicago?" they screamed, and voices of my own screamed back, "Don't give me a hard time! They've been talking about Chicago for a whole year and where were you then!?" There was only silence. They seemed to have no answer to this. The mounts went onto the walls without further problems.

As we worked I told stories. I told the crew stories about lights and about film and I told stories about bellyaches and blizzards and "self-cleaning ovens." Everyone was delighted, completely fascinated, and over lunch one day someone said they'd be really disappointed if the lights didn't go out or something. I did not stop to think before answering, "I wouldn't wait for them to perform for you like circus animals," I said a little more abruptly than I might have liked. "No one here has done anything for them, so I wouldn't stand around waiting for them to do something for you either." There was silence at the lunch table. I heard myself saying these things and I also heard my mind scolding. "You're being rude and they think you're crazy besides!" But it was too late, the words had been said.

I suggested strongly that we install Uenuku first. I could not insist that the people feel something they did not feel, but on this issue I was firm. I did not care if they thought I was crazy. We arranged the installation around Uenuku. On the Monday morning we were to begin, three people brought offerings for Uenuku. Someone had gone to the florist for a carnation and Cap had cut a shoot off the spider plant in her office. I myself had pulled a branch off a plant upstairs in Stanley Field Hall when the guard wasn't looking. There was nothing green within 200 miles of Chicago at that time of year.

The usual silence followed Uenuku's raising. No one ever seemed to be able to do anything but stare. He filled the room. We stood around him for a few quiet moments and then went to install Pukaki—a flashy operation involving a lot of people and equipment with many tense moments and a great deal of discussion. When Pukaki was finally seated up on his pedestal it was time for the morning break.

The crew began to trickle back about twenty minutes later, one of them carrying a beautiful waxy green branch. "Where did you get that, Jim?" I asked. "I had to look everywhere for something this morning." He said it was really strange, but on his way back from break he had found it. "It was lying on the floor in the corridor," he said. It had been freshly cut but he could see no plants around. "I brought it for him," he said, nodding towards Pukaki. He put the branch at the figure's feet.

And that is how it began in Chicago. Later that morning we began to install another large figure. I could not make the mount fit, which seemed strange—it had always fit before. Finally the mount went on and a technician began drilling into the pedestal so we could insert the mount. The drill stopped. "Get me the other drill," Jeff said. "We have a better drill than this." After a moment of drilling the chuck fell off the better drill. No one spoke for a few seconds until Mike broke the silence. "That can't happen," he said. "I've never seen that happen to a drill before. It's factory assembled." "Well, it just happened," said Jeff, holding the front end of the drill in his other hand. My mind cast around for the answer, for whatever information was trying to get through, but I could not hear it.

The third and last drill in the tool case was brought and finally the holes were drilled. Jeff changed to a screwdriver bit and picked up a screw to fasten the mount to the pedestal. He looked up at me now. There was shock on his face, amazement. "Something really weird is going on," he said. "There are no slots in this screw!" He held it up. It was blank and flat across the top. People were starting to shake their heads now and others wandered over to see what was happening.

"He's trying to tell you something, you fool!" said a voice in my head, but I could not tell what it was. Jeff persevered and finally the tall figure of an ancestor stood, fastened to the pedestal. I touched him and he swayed wildly. And then I knew. "Did anyone tighten the bolts on the bottom of the mount?" I asked and everyone shook their heads. We had, of course, to reverse the whole process—all the way to the beginning—and take the mount off. As we did this I smiled to myself. He had just been stalling for time until someone noticed. But no one had noticed, not even me. I promised to pay more attention.

The head of the exhibition department had seen that we were having trouble. He drew me aside now with a serious face. "Listen," he said quietly, "do you think the piece is unhappy where we're trying to put him?" I laughed in delight, I wanted to hug this man.

"No, Don," I said, "I think he was a bit nervous at first, but he's fine now." Don nodded, satisfied.

That is the way it began in Chicago. By the second week of installation I joked that we would have to bring in a load of topsoil if any more greenery appeared in the exhibition hall.

Molly Wilson, the New Zealand Vice Consul from New York, introduced me to a reporter, Andrew Webb. A New Zealander who had been living in Chicago for some years, Andrew wanted to write an article about me for a Chicago newspaper. Several times while we were installing, Andrew came to the museum to watch, to take pictures and ask questions.

On the first day, with pad and pencil in hand, Andrew asked how seriously I thought people took this "superstition stuff." In true surprise I said I would never have thought of calling it superstition and that we all took it very seriously. He looked at me a bit skeptically, maybe a bit condescendingly, and asked what I *would* call it, then. I had expected to be asked, and over breakfast had cast around in my mind for the right way to explain the way I felt. The answer, it turned out, was in the science section of my newspaper that morning. The article said that researchers had just discovered that elephants communicate by using a low-frequency sound vibration emanating from their foreheads. The sound is below the range of human hearing and scientists had previously been unaware of it. This, the article said with great excitement, could explain the mystery of how elephants find each other from miles away.

"Look," I now said to Andrew, "elephants are some of the oldest mammals on the planet. We've even raised them in captivity for centuries and it took us until 1986 to find out that they have another way of talking to each other? Just because we haven't yet found a way to measure something, a way to document it, we say it's not scientifically possible! We call it a mystery or a superstition. I, for one, do not need to wait another 50 or 1000 years until a smart human figures out a way to document and measure the energy that transfers from an artist into the art while it's being made. I am saying, Andrew, that as far as I'm concerned, this *is* science. We just don't know enough about it yet."

Andrew had not interrupted. Now he looked around the exhibition hall. He looked at Pukaki looming over us and said, "I understand what you're saying."

Andrew had lived in Dunedin, in New Zealand's South Island, for eighteen years. He said he'd been to the Otago Museum there possibly a hundred times and must have seen many of these same Maori objects before. "I never noticed them there," he said. "I wonder why they have so much more power here?" He suggested that perhaps they were out of context and therefore looked more unique, but I disagreed. Field Museum had collections of very similar material and even owned a significant number of Maori pieces. They really were not so out of context. He wanted to know, then, what my theory was and I explained, wondering how he would accept it. These objects, I told him, had been in New Zealand museums for over a hundred years in many cases. Some had been in storage chambers, others on display, but all in some way had been locked away. The Maori people rarely, if ever, went to the museums. The people who did go looked at the pieces simply as objects hanging on the wall. As the years passed, the pieces were no longer called by name. They were no longer caressed and no further words and stories clothed them. They became in a sense dormant.

Then a curator from America went to New Zealand. He spoke to curators there and they began to point to certain carvings. They began to talk about them and ask questions about them and over time, 174 of these dormant pieces were chosen. The people in the museums began to pull the pieces out of storage. They dusted them and prepared them. Soon a conservator and a registrar from America arrived. Elders, perhaps for the first time, entered the museums and called their ancestors by name again. There were ceremonies held for them, prayers said over them and when everyone went home, there were stories told about the 174 who had been chosen. "They began to wake up," I said to Andrew. "They began to wake up and then they came to America, where there were more ceremonies and more adventures and more words and stories to clothe them. No wonder they are more powerful now. They will go back to New Zealand and take that power to the others, to the ones who were left behind."

Andrew nodded his head. I couldn't really tell what he felt about this. I was pleased to see, though, that after a few days with us at the museum he looked thoughtful instead of skeptical, intrigued instead of condescending.

Field Museum, the only natural history museum on the tour, had a different plan for the opening ceremony. The Maori people had so far been called in at dawn by museum officials. Field Museum said that if these were the first peoples of New

Zealand, they must be greeted by the first peoples of America. They invited a band of Nisgáa Indians from the American Northwest to stage a formal challenge to the entering Maoris. The group was to be led by the Nisgáa, who had some years before carved the 65-foot totem pole that stands in front of Field Museum.

The publicist at the museum said CBS wanted to talk to me. They had been told about my stories and wanted to hear more. I said no. I was as surprised as she at my response, since I so loved to tell the stories. But as soon as the question was asked I knew I could not tell them to the press. In that moment I realized that my commitment to the Maori people had been a very personal one and that I wanted to tell the elders these stories myself. I did not want them to read these wonderful adventures, now part of their history, in two-inch headlines in the *Chicago Sun Times* or hear them on TV. The publicist was disappointed but respected this. I was not asked again.

I became friends with Andrew Webb and his wife Jan during the time he was gathering material for the article. As with everyone else, I loved telling them about Te Maori and did so, casually and spontaneously, over brunch or dinner or to Andrew as he observed at the museum. They invited me out to combine my interview with dinner at a Thai restaurant. Once the meal was ordered, Andrew put his tape recorder on the table. He asked me about truck rides and freighter planes, about packing and insurance and about my background. Finally, he asked me to tell again one of the stories about the lights going out.

I was having such a good time by then I forgot. I forgot that there was a tape recorder on the table and that I was no longer talking to a friend but to a reporter. I began the tale and soon noticed a pain in my stomach. I had simply eaten too much, I thought, and went on with the story. The pain grew worse. I did not tell Andrew and Jan because they would be concerned, but soon had to excuse myself to the bathroom where I unbuttoned my waistband. It didn't help. I came back and continued talking, trying to ignore the now fierce pain in my belly. A wave of nausea rolled over me and I stopped talking, holding onto the edge of the table.

"Are you all right?" Jan asked, alarmed. "You're turning colors in front of us!" I said that in fact, I seemed to be very sick. I was so dizzy I could hardly think, could hardly remain upright. Andrew went quickly to get the car.

Within two minutes of getting into the car I was fine and knew in a flash what had happened. "Look," I said, "I'm really 100% OK now and I know what happened back there." They looked at me, disbelieving, amazed, but aware that I now seemed well. "I wasn't supposed to be telling you that story," I said. I explained and they were stunned that this could have happened. "Then I won't touch it," Andrew said immediately. "Are you *sure* you're feeling all right?" Jan asked once more. "Really," I said, "let's go out for dessert!"

That weekend I went to their house for brunch. As he drove me to the station afterwards, Andrew said, "You know, every time you hear about these strange things they're always happening to somebody else. Then," he said with some glee, "you almost died right in front of us the other night!" "Gee, thanks, Andrew," I said drily, "I'm glad you enjoyed it."

We were approaching the end of the installation. One of the technicians began to set the lights starting at the front of the hall with Pukaki. The first light he clipped into the track didn't work. He took one that was already lit, one he knew worked, from another part of the room and clipped it in. The light went on—and then fell apart in his hands. The third one he tried didn't work at all and the fourth flared briefly before the bulb blew.

Someone mentioned to me then that there was a bit of trouble with the lights up at the front of the hall. "Well, it's late on a Friday so let's not deal with it now," I said. "If you continue to have trouble on Monday morning come and get me." We all looked at Pukaki and at the four broken lamps. They asked what it was I intended to do. I looked surprised. "I'll have a talk with him," I said.

I planned to get in early Monday before anyone arrived but there was no need. On the weekend Pukaki came to me in a dream. We stood and cried together. "I know, I know," I said. "I'm tired too. I too want to go home. But we are here now and we must do this one more time. You must let them put the lights on you one more time and then you must stand and look proud and fierce for all the people who will come to visit. Just one more time you must listen to all the silly things they will say about you because they think you cannot hear." Fat tears rolled down his cheeks and he said he didn't know if he could. He didn't know if he had the strength or the courage. I said he had to find it somewhere inside him and then, when it was done here, I would take him home. He promised to try and I asked him to talk to the others for me. I said it was too draining, too exhausting for me to talk to each of them as I had to him and that he must tell them all to behave. He said he would and we hugged each other. Then I woke up.

On Monday the lights worked fine. "I must have been doing something wrong on Friday," the technician said, "because they're working now." I agreed that was probably the case.

*　　　*　　　*　　　*　　　*

When dawn arrives in Chicago it arrives over the lake. At first light, drumbeats could be heard from inside the building. The drums grew louder and the voice of a woman rang out—in the Nisgáa language this time—and as she called, she waved them in. Behind her the Nisgáa braves hopped from foot to foot, their beaver helmets dancing. The Maori elders began to make their way in slow procession up the steps. At the head of the procession were two men and a woman, all wearing feather cloaks. The woman was the Maori Queen.

Drums beat louder now as the Maori group appeared, framed in the door against the pale morning sky. Maori warriors went

forward to meet the challenging Nisgáa and I could not breathe
as these people approached each other. I could not know what
their eyes saw or what their hearts felt as these first peoples
greeted each other for the first time. But I knew, in the charged,
dancing electricity of the great hall that they were really the
same peoples and that we were the same peoples as they.

The sound was louder now as the warriors danced up against
each other, challenged and then made their peace. The Nisgáa
braves threw down their weapons and the procession of Maori
elders was allowed to pass. The Nisgáa followed.

Outside, the sun rose over the lake and as it did, a procession
of beautiful people with joy and wonder on their faces moved
slowly down the stairs. There they would greet their ancestors
who waited silently and with fierce pride.

SIX

The Fruit

My cousin, Bob:

"So what are you saying? That this is the one true religion?"

"Good grief! Are you kidding? It has nothing to do with religion."

"What then?"

"It has to do with intuition and . . . and with human energy, I guess. It has to do with people who haven't forgotten there are other ways of gathering information."

A friend:

"Is it only Maori artifacts?"

"Well, right now it seems to be focused on Maori artifacts but I think that's only because these pieces have come from a living culture of people who still believe in them. I don't think the Egyptian pieces, or the Northwest Coast American Indian material or any art I've worked with has had any less power or meant any less to the people who made it. It's just that no one has listened to those in a long time. They've been too long separated from anyone who will let them speak."

Another friend:

"This is pretty strange stuff."

"But I'm telling you, it isn't strange at all. It was ordinary, everyday stuff."

                                                  May 2, 1986, New York

Lesley Abernethy
Auckland, N.Z.

Dear Lesley,

Some wonderful things have been happening. Remember I told you that Field Museum invited a band of Nisgáa Indians to greet the Maori elders at the dawn ceremony in Chicago on March 6? Well, the head of the Nisgáa band is a well-known carver. He carved the 65-foot totem pole that stands permanently in front of Field Museum. Anyway, the Nisgáa carvers started talking to the Maori carvers who had come up from New Zealand to give demonstrations at Field Museum during the exhibition. They enjoyed each other so much and found so much in common that they began talking about the possibility of a carving exchange—the Nisgáa would carve a 65-foot totem pole to be raised in New Zealand and the Maoris maybe a 65-foot canoe or something like that to be given to the Nisgáa in Vancouver, where they live. That's when they came to me—at the evening reception for Te Maori at Field Museum. Word has gotten out that I specialize in moving big things around the world.

Well, I was very excited about the idea and suggested we ship the trees and send the carvers to live among each other while the carving is going on. But I'm a bit worn out right now after all these years of working like a fiend and didn't feel up to jumping on a new project of this size just yet. I figured I'd wait till I get to New Zealand in June and start exploring the idea a bit then (slowly). That's not the way things happened.

When I got back to New York I mentioned the carving exchange idea to a film-maker friend of mine who won the Academy Award for best documentary film a few years ago. He was very excited by the idea. Two days later he mentioned it to the National Geographic Society for whom he is making another film. They were very excited by it. I get the feeling I'm supposed to take this project on or that it has taken me on. I've now been working out how to ship ten-ton cedar trees from Vancouver to New Zealand and some equivalent totara trees from New Zealand to Vancouver. ("Don't you ever do anything normal?" asks my customs broker when I asked him to research this. I told him I try not to. It is very boring.)

In the meantime, I'm going nuts trying to organize the final details of Te Maori's return home. I have to make trucks meet up with planes meet up with couriers meet up with customs documents and other planes and all this with only a month to go. Frenzy.

I'll be landing in Auckland with the first shipment and transferring right to a truck to go on to Wellington so I'll call you a few days later from there. See you soon!

Love,
Carol

My friend Deborah:

"I don't believe this—now give me the details again, slowly. I can hardly understand you, you're talking so fast."

"OK, OK, I'll slow down. It's just that this one even has *me* freaked out. I was writing stories in my journal last night. I was writing about the adventure when the first truck with Te Maori on board left New York for St. Louis in January of 1985. It was a terrible winter and the driver, Joe, called me at 4:30 A.M., waking me out of a dead sleep to tell me the climate control unit had gelled up and the temperature was falling. I wrote that much of the story last night and then went to bed. At 4:30 this morning my phone rang. The minute I opened my eyes and saw my digital clock glowing 4:30 in the dark I knew something really weird was happening. That paragraph I'd written the night before was just too fresh in my mind. I picked up the phone and it was Joe! I haven't spoken to him in eight or nine months and the incident I was writing about took place a year and a half ago!

"Joe couldn't figure out how I knew his voice so quick—he'd only said two words—and was shocked when I told him."

"It *is* really eerie, but why was he calling you now? Did he have another one of your shipments on his truck?"

"That's the hilarious part. After I got over my shock I asked where he was. 'I'm on 60th and Broadway,' he says, 'and I'm comin' to take you to breakfast.' I mentioned that it was 4:30 in the morning and asked if he was going to give me time to get up. 'I'll drive slow,' he says. So I hang up and leap out of bed to wash my face and throw on jeans and a shirt and this 45-foot tractor trailer pulls up in front of my apartment building. I climbed in and we cruised Lexington Avenue until we found a greasy spoon coffee shop open at that hour."

"And this was all this morning?"

"Yes. We talked for hours and I've just come back from breakfast. I suppose I should try to go back to bed but I'm too jazzed up to sleep."

June 20, 1986, Los Angeles

Doris and Bernie Stowens,
New York

Dear Doris and Bernie,

I'm sitting on a Te Maori crate in the cargo terminal at the L.A. airport and will very likely be sitting here another seven hours. That is how long the foreman says it will be before we actually load the pallets and tow them out to the plane. I will have crate ridges in my backside by then. At least I've got some good company—the New Zealand conservator who will be taking over my role for the New Zealand tour of the exhibition. He has been working with me in Chicago for the past two weeks as we packed up the show for the last time and is sitting on a neighboring crate. Anyway, pull up a chair and get yourself a cup of coffee . . . you have to hear this last extraordinary thing that happened as we were loading the truck in Chicago two days ago.

About two weeks before I left New York a telex from New Zealand came through AFA. It requested that the three trucks, en route from Auckland to Wellington (the final leg of the journey), deviate to Maori maraes along the way so that they could be ceremonially greeted by the elders. I knew our indemnity board would never approve such a thing but I submitted it anyway and sure enough, they turned it down as too dangerous. For some reason, maybe that I was under too much pressure to get all the other logistics organized, I just sent a reply back to New Zealand saying it had been turned down and was, therefore, not possible. Thank you very much. End of story. I went on with my work assuming the matter was closed.

We were well into loading the first truck at Field Museum the day before yesterday when an urgent telex came through from Wellington. It said they had gotten my reply and it was unacceptable. It said the return of Te Maori was regarded as the triumphant return of a hero and that the Maori people could not be denied the opportunity to properly greet their ancestors. The compromise position they offered was that the trucks would not deviate from the main route but that groups of elders would follow the trucks and perform ceremonies along the way. This sounds better but isn't. I knew our indemnity board was not going to approve this either and with good reason! If a car comes around the bend and hits the truck pulled over on a narrow shoulder on a winding road in the middle of the night . . . well, the indemnity board would say, what were you doing sitting on a narrow shoulder on a winding road in the middle of the night? That wasn't part of the plan.

While Jeanne Hedstrom and I were reading this telex and tearing our hair out in front of Field Museum, Joe McGinley, the truck driver, walked over and said, "The truck is dead. Everything, completely dead." "Oh, great," I thought, forgetting the telex in the face of this new disaster. Joe tried to jump-start the motor and instead, the battery caught fire. He leaped out and clamped a towel over the flames, yelling at me to cover my eyes in case it exploded. "What do you think it is?" I asked when the fire was out. "Well, why don't we say it's the starter so I can feel better," said Joe, "but we both know what it is!" I nodded and we laughed. "Why don't you get up in the trailer and *do* something about it?" he said.

I did. I climbed up into the truck with the crates while Joe tinkered around with the engine. I walked around, a little impatient at first, and spoke with Uenuku and Pukaki and the others. "Come on, guys," I said. "We don't have time for this nonsense today. We have a plane to catch." I felt no response. "We're going home now," I said and waited. Still, I felt nothing. Then, suddenly, my mind went back to the telex and I felt a little jolt, a little energy in the truck. I could just feel them all glaring at me, hurt and upset that I could have been so cold and unfeeling. "OK, OK," I said. "It's the telex, isn't it? I promise you, I'll find a way for you to be greeted by your people all the way from Auckland to Wellington. I'll lie to the indemnity board and say I never saw the telex. Then I can pretend I don't see the cars following us and can be surprised when these groups of people stop the truck along the way. I can treat it as an unexpected, emergency procedure. Come *on,* guys," I said, "stop pouting! I promise you I'll find a way to do it." The floor of the truck rumbled. The engine had started. I poked my head out the side and smiled at Joe. "Can I come out now?" I called. He grinned and gave me an OK sign.

I'll let you know what happens. I know I'm taking a huge risk here but I didn't know what else to do. Also, I can't wait to see what goes on once this exhibition starts to tour New Zealand. It opens on August 16 at the National Museum in Wellington. The emotional build-up these last two years has been incredible and by then, on its home ground, the opening should be electric!

Love,
Carol

In the distance now I can see a strip of land. Soon it is hidden by clouds. Tears spring to my eyes and I brush them away. I cross my legs, uncross them, curl sideways in the seat and then sit straight. The tears have come and gone, without warning, without reason, since Los Angeles. I hug my knees and laugh.

Beside me sits a colleague from New Zealand who will soon take my place. For two weeks, in Chicago, I have told this man everything. He has seen the exhibition come down for the last time in America. He has seen the exhibition packed for the last time in America and he has learned from me, all that he will need to know for the next two years as it makes its tour of New Zealand. Sometimes, as I pointed out to be cautious of that splinter, to watch carefully while fastening that lid, this brace; sometimes then, a small voice would crawl up in the back of my mind. "Soon it will be the end for you," it said. I pushed the voice away and went on, joyously, with my work. We were going home.

Now we are on our way. I have noted at what point the enormous, plastic-draped pallet went into the belly of the plane and I know that if I leave my seat and walk back two emergency exit doors on the right side of the plane, I will be standing directly over Uenuku's crate. I do this. I stand in the middle of the aisle and stare blankly at the floor. The flight attendant asks me to take my seat, we will be landing soon.

On the ground, not far away and through the scuttling clouds, something else is happening where I cannot see. A group of Maori elders has gathered, about fifty of them, mostly dressed in black. They move cautiously, tentatively, and are unsure of themselves in the restricted parts of an airport. Slowly, they are gathered and then escorted through a security door and onto the tarmac. They have been given special clearance and are taken out to where they can see the runway. They stand at the point to which the plane will taxi once it slows and turns. Electricity ripples through the crowd now. They are told that the pilot has made radio contact and the plane will touch down on time. Fifty faces turn upwards and peer into the sky, searching, piercing the clouds. They see nothing. A wind comes up and the sky threatens rain. The crowd looks tiny in the hugeness of the tarmac. They huddle together, draw their feather cloaks, coats and black sweaters tightly around them. In the air, not far away and through the scuttling clouds, something else is happening where they cannot see.

The head purser has come and moved us to the front of the plane. A security escort will be there, he says, as soon as the doors are opened, and will take me and my colleague planeside where we can see the pallet come off. The purser has been told who we are and what we carry.

I am calmer now. We are below the clouds and I watch the sea, the sheep, the rolling hills and tiny houses tucked here and there into the green. This is New Zealand and I am coming home. I am bringing friends. A new seatmate asks if I have been to New Zealand before and I say yes. We talk but I don't know about what. I stare at my hands on the arms of the chair and think that they must be someone else's. My breathing is even. Outside the windows, hills and sheep, houses and airport buildings blur into one as we move faster, drop lower, move faster, dipping slightly to the right and then the left. I am not breathing at all now and my seatmate talks on. I wait, rigid, knowing that now, any second now, soon, and then I feel it. The wheels touch down. We bounce, ever so slightly and then touch down again, on New Zealand soil. My head falls back against the seat and I begin to laugh as tears leap to my eyes. My colleague quietly squeezes my arm because he knows. I smile at him.

On the ground, not far away, something has been happening that I cannot see. A large group that looks small stares in awe as an enormous silver plane drops below the clouds. There is a murmur, some excitement and some confusion. They are assured that this is the one and with that assurance, all eyes turn to the sky once more. The plane drops lower. Wheels glide gently out of its belly and the people huddled on the tarmac watch in silence as the plane moves faster, drops lower, moves faster. It dips slightly to the right and then to the left. There is a great deal of noise now and a great deal of activity on the tarmac as the airport crew prepares for the plane's arrival. The group in black does not notice. Their breathing is even. They wait, rigid, knowing that now, any second now, soon and then they see it. The wheels touch down. A woman's voice pierces the air. A shrill greeting call rips from her throat and blends with the noise of the jet. The plane races past them, roaring to slow itself and the eerie wail follows it to the end of the runway. Her voice carries and blends all the anguish and all the joy and all the fear that have gone with her ancestors to America. The men's voices join her now. The elders begin their prayers and as the plane slows, turns and begins to taxi back towards them, the people begin to cry.

*   *   *   *   *

It is night time and there is thick fog. Occasionally I say a few words to the driver, or he to me. We do not know each other and we talk of small, inconsequential things. I have been up for two days now. I am very tired and try to sleep but the roads are too winding and too slippery, the fog too thick, the cargo too precious. I am tense. I close my eyes and they open again.

Close behind us is an unmarked police car with two plain-clothes policemen. They too are tense. The roads are deserted, the occasional town still and unwelcoming. I am keenly aware of the police car. Often I glance in the mirror to be sure it is still there. It will be ten hours to Wellington.

Close behind the police car is a mini-bus. It is filled with elders and close behind the mini-bus is a car, also filled with elders. I am keenly aware of the bus and the car but pretend that I am not. These are the people about whom I am not supposed to know. "Slow down a little," I say to the driver, "the elders are falling behind." He nods.

Now we are coasting off onto a narrow shoulder along the side of a winding road. "Where are we?" I ask. "Taupiri," he says and this means nothing to me until he adds, "the resting place of the kings." I open my door but do not get out. I perch there, high up in the cab of the truck, waiting, watching, wondering how I will explain to the indemnity board what we are doing here if something goes wrong. The police pull up behind. They keep their headlights on and stand beside the truck. It is very black out and the fog very thick. The elders begin, stiffly, to climb out of the bus and the car. It is 2 A.M. and they are not used to driving all night in the fog. Some are very, very old and I wonder how it is possible that they can do this. I sit on my perch and watch. I do not want to intrude because I am a foreigner but one of the women comes forward and motions me to climb down.

Before us, in the night, on the other side of a railroad track, are two hills and above, a fuzzy moon. The woman tucks my hand under her arm. "A train is coming," someone says. "That's alright," she answers, "we can get across before it comes." She pulls me onto the tracks. They are wide and we must hurry and from the corner of my eye I see strange flashes of pink. I look closer in the night. The woman has gotten out of the car—black hair, dark face, black coat, black stockings and on her feet, fuzzy pink bedroom slippers. The pink slippers pump up and down, disembodied. They climb over the steel rails, crunch on the gravel in between and then we are across. We wait. The elders do not begin because they do not want to be interrupted by the train but when one does not come, they do begin. One of them calls into the night. He calls to the white grave markers that dot the two hills. The graves float, lumines-cent in the blackness, and the hoarse, emotional voice screams into the night fog. A strange feeling begins to crawl in my body and then the train comes, rocket, rocket, rocket, whistle, whooooshhh . . . it is gone and the elder continues as if there had been no train.

Now, the woman feels me shudder with cold. She opens her coat; this woman with a wide face, a face that wears every-thing—all that she thinks and all that she feels, all that she knows—on the outside. This woman with a face that keeps nothing back, wraps me into her coat with her. She locks her arms around my chest. Her body presses and warms my back, her arms and her coat warm my front. She is rocking softly back and forth, keening. A tall, old, old man steps forward. He is bent and stooped but thumps his walking stick with great force on the wet grass. He screams shrilly into the night, waves his stick at the graves and then at the truck waiting by the side of the road. The woman whispers in my ear that these are the graves of the very kings we carry in the truck. She tells me that they are greeting each other and as I look back and forth, from one to the other, my skin prickles with something I cannot name. We climb back into the cars and the truck and the mini-bus. We drive on, and twice more we stop in the night.

*   *   *   *   *

It is the end for me. Some weeks have gone by. One last time I have lifted them gently from their crates. I have inspected them carefully, with the man who will take my place as they travel through their own country. Together, with painstaking attention, this man and I have agreed that the pieces remain in the same condition in which they were lent some years before. One by one we have signed the pieces of paper that confirm this. We have smiled and wagged our heads that so much time could already have passed. It is the end for me.

I sit, this evening, on the same marae, in the same museum where four years before a small wooden figure was ceremonially placed in my care. Tonight I will ceremonially return that same small wooden figure as a symbol of the return of them all. The American Ambassador is speaking. He is making a long and very pleasant speech and I become slightly concerned. I have not prepared a speech even though it is I who am expected next at the podium. I had not expected things to be so formal but I tell myself not to worry, it is not my way to give prepared speeches.

I look around now and am pleased. The feeling tonight is austere. There are many government people in dark, conservative suits. They sit in a horse-shoe facing the marae in straight-backed chairs. It is all very clinical, severe. It is all somehow very bare and I am pleased because it is not an atmosphere in which I am likely to cry. I was afraid I might cry.

It is my turn now. I stand and smile at the people and say hello. I say what mixed feelings I have and that I am speaking also for my colleagues in New York, for those who could not be here. I tell how very, very proud we are to have been part of this, how with all our vision we could not have had the vision to see the impact that Te Maori would have. Then I say I am also relieved and they all smile. I say I have inspected all the pieces one last time and that they are fine but are no longer . . . and then it crawls up in the back of my throat . . . my responsibility. I pause, look down and try to hold it together. The people are waiting for me to go on. "I am also very sad," I say slowly and carefully and then I can no longer hold it. My face crumples and I begin to cry. I try to smile, to talk through my tears and can't. "OK!" I laugh now and slap the podium. "I have to stop this!" I keep talking even as I cry. I say I have come to love the people and the land and all of the little wooden friends on the other side of the wall. Many are crying with me now, man and woman, Maori and Pakeha alike. I watch them and it helps me go on. I say I hope this will be a transition for me rather than an ending and that only with that in mind will I have the courage to hand back the beautiful little fellow who is waiting.

Carefully, I lift him from the table behind me. With a shaky smile I walk quickly forward and place him in the arms of the Minister of Maori Affairs. Then I go back to my seat and begin, quietly, to weep.

It is nearly dawn. We stand, a very large group, on the steps in front of the National Museum. They tell me six hundred have been invited. There is some vagueness and confusion as the elders work out who should be in front, who to the left and who behind. Then it is time. It is first light and dawn begins to creep into the Wellington sky. A call rings out, a woman's voice in the almost-blackness. The crowd begins to move forward. We follow the elders, shuffle up the steps, into the building, past the long canoes and up another set of steps. Then we enter the room where Pukaki waits, Pukeroa looks on and around the other side of the wall, Uenuku stands in the center.

The elders and officials assemble and the speeches begin. They speak, one after the other, in Maori. There are songs and more speeches, prayers, some laughter and then it is done. Te Maori is declared officially opened and the New Zealand tour has begun.

I stand a moment longer in surprise, then shrug my shoulders and leave the room. I feel empty and vaguely sad and as I make my way with the crowd to the breakfast, I wonder if it is only me. I wonder if some mood I am in has made me miss the electricity, the emotion that must surely have filled the room. One of the elders is at my side now, one who has been to some of the openings in America. "There wasn't the same feeling here," he says, a little sad, a little bewildered. "It was the hosts that made it happen there," he says and then I know that yes, it is true. When everyone is the same there is no electricity. It is opposites together that make it happen. Here, they were nearly all the same so though they made speeches and sang songs, though they chanted and prayed, though it looked the same as all the ones before, it was not the same as all the ones before. The energy of these people today was not bouncing off and mingling with an opposite and equally intense energy, and so the energy of these people today diffused and disappeared.

So the future lies in opposites, or at least in the different coming together. This I know because now another man stands at my elbow. Yesterday I sat with this man in a room. He is a carver, a carver who some months before in Chicago met a carver of a different culture. These two men spoke and as they spoke there was a flash, a spark of electricity, and from the spark jumped a little flame. So yesterday, a few of us sat in a room and talked and when we finished, a new and exciting project had been officially launched. Excitement ran very high in the room where I sat with this man and others yesterday. Now, he stands at my elbow and gives me a kiss on the cheek. "It looks good!" he says and I say yes and mention something about Te Maori. He pauses, confused and then says, "No, not that. *Our* thing from yesterday, the carving exchange!" He goes on to say how he has approached the Minister about getting a tree and how favorable was the response and there, suddenly as he speaks, is a flash of life, a flash of electricity.

So the future lies in opposites and I see, as he talks excitedly that I have come four years down a long road to learn this: Te Maori has planted a seed.